CLASSICAL ITALIAN COOKING

Beryl Frank

CHARTWELL
BOOKS, INC.

introduction

Classical Italian cuisine is hearty and varied and can now be found almost anywhere in the world. It is based predominantly on the indigenous products of the many regions of Italy—ranging from sunny islands to mountainous countrysides.

Pasta, a must in Italian meal-planning, comes in many intriguing shapes and sizes. If you choose to cook pasta in the Italian manner, you must first understand the term *al dente*. In English it means firm to the bite. In cooking it means less cooking time than for soft, mushy pasta. Firm *al dente* pasta is the Italian style.

Before planning to cook a classic Italian recipe, it would be wise to spend some time at the pasta section of your grocery store. If there are only one or two commercial pastas on the shelf, find your nearest Italian grocery store. Familiarize yourself with what is available, then start trying recipes. If you really have the cooking bug, begin by making your own pasta at home. Either way, plan to enjoy the new taste treats and the compliments you will receive when you cook Italian.

Basically, three kinds of pasta are used. The first, of course, is spaghetti. The easiest way to think of spaghetti is to visualize a length of cord or string. This pasta is round and solid and includes capellini, fedelini, vermicelli, spaghettini, spaghetti, and spaghettoni, varying in thickness from very thin to quite thick.

Macaronis are round and hollow. As with spaghetti there are many different and fascinating kinds and shapes of macaronis, with one thing in common—all are hollow pasta.

Noodles, another general classification for pasta, include many different widths, ranging from as small as one-eighth of an inch to the extra-broad lasagna.

Most of the ingredients necessary for fine Italian cooking are available at local grocery stores. Buy with care, and buy fresh—then cook. Sit back and listen as the compliments flow.

Thanks to the many excellent cooks who shared their recipes here. Thanks also to my lovable, capable editor, who helped in so many ways—and to Lou, who is lovable, too.

Published by

CHARTWELL BOOKS, INC.
A Division of BOOK SALES, INC.
110 Enterprise Avenue
Secaucus, New Jersey 07094

Copyright © 1984 Ottenheimer Publishers, Inc.
All rights reserved.
Printed in Hong Kong.
ISBN: 0-89009-776-3

Designed by Phillip A. Mullen
Photography by Greg Holmes
Food Stylist: Nella DeVitto

contents

Introduction   6

Antipasti   8

Soups   12

Salads   16

Pasta, Rice, and Grain   20

Poultry   36

Fish   50

Meats   66

Vegetables   82

Breads   86

Desserts   88

Index   92

antipasti

stuffed artichokes

Yield: 4 servings

4 medium globe artichokes
¾ cup dry bread crumbs
3 tablespoons grated Parmesan
  cheese

1 tablespoon chopped parsley
½ teaspoon garlic salt
¼ teaspoon crumbled dried
  oregano

¼ teaspoon pepper
2 tablespoons butter
2 tablespoons olive oil
1 cup boiling water

Remove stems from artichokes. Cut about ½ inch from tips of leaves, using kitchen shears. Drop into boiling salted water; cook 5 minutes. Drain; shake to remove water; cool.

Combine bread crumbs, cheese, parsley, garlic salt, oregano, and pepper; mix well.

Tap bases of artichokes on a flat surface to spread the leaves. Stuff each artichoke with ¼ of bread crumb mixture; spoon it between the leaves. Put artichokes into a saucepan or stove-top casserole; place them close together so they do not tip over. Top each artichoke with ½ tablespoon butter and ½ tablespoon oil. Pour in boiling water; cover. Cook over low heat 35 to 45 minutes or until artichokes are tender.

mozzarella cheese sandwiches with anchovy sauce

Yield: 8 (3-inch) sandwiches; 4 servings

anchovy sauce

¼ cup butter
2 anchovy fillets
1 tablespoon chopped drained capers

2 tablespoons chopped parsley
Juice of ½ lemon

Melt butter in small skillet; do not brown.

Rinse anchovies under cold running water; chop finely. Add with capers and parsley to butter. Add lemon juice; stir well. Keep sauce warm.

mozarella cheese sandwiches

16 thin slices of Italian bread (½
  inch thick)
8 thick slices mozzarella cheese
  (3/8 inch thick)

3 eggs
Salt to taste
½ cup dry bread crumbs
¼ cup butter or margarine

Remove crusts from bread. Lay 1 cheese slice between 2 bread slices; press together.

In a small bowl beat eggs and a pinch of salt. Dip bread and cheese sandwiches into egg; dredge in bread crumbs.

Heat butter over moderate heat in a heavy skillet. Add cheese sandwiches. Cook until golden brown on one side; turn and cook on other side. Serve immediately topped with anchovy sauce.

clams casino

Yield: 6 servings

2 dozen cherrystone clams
2 tablespoons olive oil
1 tablespoon butter
½ cup finely minced onion
¼ cup finely chopped green pepper

2 cloves garlic, peeled, chopped
1 cup dry bread crumbs
4 slices crisp bacon, crumbled
½ teaspoon crumbled dried
  oregano

2 tablespoons grated Parmesan
  cheese
Parsley flakes and paprika
Olive oil

Wash and scrub clams well to remove grit. Place on a baking sheet. Put into 450°F oven until shells open. Remove meat from shells; chop. Reserve chopped clams; discard ½ of shells.

Heat 2 tablespoons oil and the butter in a small skillet. Add onion, pepper, and garlic; sauté until tender. Remove from heat; cool. Add bread crumbs, bacon, oregano, cheese, and reserved clams; mix well. Fill clam shells with mixture. Sprinkle with parsley flakes and paprika. Drizzle with olive oil. Bake in 450°F oven until lightly browned (about 7 minutes). Serve hot.

opposite: stuffed artichokes

stuffed olives

Yield: 6 servings

1 (6-ounce) can jumbo pitted black
  olives
1 (2-ounce) can anchovy fillets
2 tablespoons olive oil
1 clove garlic, minced

2 tablespoons finely chopped
  parsley
12 stemmed cherry tomatoes
½ medium green pepper, thinly
  sliced

Drain olives.

Drain anchovy fillets; cut each in half. Stuff each olive with ½ anchovy fillet. Place in serving bowl.

Combine oil, garlic, and parsley. Pour over olives; mix well. Chill several hours. Bring to room temperature before serving.

Garnish with cherry tomatoes and green peppers. Be sure to provide cocktail picks for spearing these nibbles.

melon with prosciutto

Yield: 4 to 6 servings, depending on number of other appetizers

½ large ripe honeydew or
  cantaloupe
¼ pound prosciutto
A pepper mill

Remove seeds and rind from melon; slice into crescents.

Cut ham slices in half. Wrap a piece of ham around each piece of melon. Arrange on a platter. Grind fresh pepper over ham and melon just before serving.

Lemon or lime wedges are a suitable garnish.

Note: Fresh ripe figs or papaya can be substituted for the melon.

stuffed mushrooms

Yield: 4 servings

1 pound medium or large
  mushrooms
1 cup dry bread crumbs
2 tablespoons dried parsley flakes
2 tablespoons grated Parmesan cheese
¼ teaspoon garlic powder
Salt and pepper
5 tablespoons olive oil, divided

Wash mushrooms well; remove stems. Hollow out mushroom caps slightly by scraping with a teaspoon. Drain well; pat dry.

Combine bread crumbs, parsley, cheese, garlic powder, salt, pepper, and 2 tablespoons olive oil; mix well. Fill mushrooms with the crumb mixture.

Pour 3 tablespoons olive oil in the bottom of a shallow baking dish. Tilt to coat dish evenly. Place mushroom caps in the oiled baking dish.

sauce

1 small onion, chopped
2 teaspoons olive oil
1 (8-ounce) can tomato sauce
½ teaspoon sugar
¼ teaspoon crumbled oregano
¼ teaspoon garlic powder
Salt and pepper

Sauté onion in oil in a small pan until tender. Add remaining ingredients; stir well. Simmer 10 minutes.

Pour sauce evenly over mushrooms. Bake at 350°F 30 minutes.

opposite: melon with prosciutto

soups

bean soup

Yield: 6 servings

2 cups dried white beans
8 cups water
1 teaspoon salt
6 tablespoons olive oil
1 large onion, chopped
½ cup diced bacon

2 cloves garlic, peeled, minced
1 stalk celery, chopped
1 carrot, peeled, chopped
4 tomatoes, peeled, coarsely
  chopped
1 teaspoon crumbled dried rosemary

1 teaspoon crumbled sweet basil
1½ cups cooked short pasta
Salt and pepper
Grated Parmesan cheese

Wash beans; pick over. Place in kettle with water; soak overnight. Add 1 teaspoon salt to beans; simmer until soft. With slotted spoon, remove ½ beans; force through sieve or food mill. Add puree to remaining beans and liquid.

Heat oil in heavy skillet. Add onion, bacon, garlic, celery, and carrot; sauté until onion is golden. Add onion mixture, tomatoes, and seasonings to beans; cook 30 minutes. Add pasta; salt and pepper to taste. Cook 10 minutes. Serve with grated Parmesan cheese.

clam soup

Yield: 4 servings

2 dozen cherrystone clams in shells
3 tablespoons olive oil
2 cloves garlic, peeled, minced
4 cups peeled ripe tomatoes, coarsely chopped

¼ cup white wine
4 tablespoons chopped Italian
  flat-leaf parsley

Scrub clams well under cold running water. Soak 30 minutes in cold water to cover.

Heat oil in large saucepan. Add garlic; sauté 1 minute. Add tomatoes and wine; bring to boil. Reduce heat to low; simmer 15 minutes. Keep warm.

In large frying pan or Dutch oven with close-fitting lid, bring 1 cup water to boil. Drain clams well; place in pan. Cover; steam 5 to 10 minutes, until clams open. (Discard any clams that will not open.) Place clams in shells in warm soup bowls.

Strain clam broth through cheesecloth; add to tomato sauce. Mix well; pour over clams in bowls. Sprinkle with parsley; serve with garlic toast.

green soup with meatballs

Yield: 4 servings

½ pound fresh spinach or beet
  greens
½ cup water
¼ teaspoon salt

Remove stems from spinach; rinse well.

In a medium saucepan, heat water and salt. Add the spinach. Reduce heat to low; cook 3 minutes. Drain well; coarsely chop.

soup

¾ pound lean ground beef
½ cup dry bread crumbs
¼ cup grated Parmesan cheese
1 egg, well-beaten

½ cup finely chopped parsley
Salt
White pepper
4 cups beef broth (homemade or canned)

In a bowl combine ground beef, bread crumbs, cheese, egg, parsley, salt, and pepper; mix well. Form into walnut-size meatballs.

In large saucepan heat beef broth to boiling. Add spinach and meatballs; bring to boil again. Reduce heat to low; cover. Simmer 15 minutes.

opposite: green soup with meatballs

neapolitan minestrone

Yield: 6 servings

1½ pounds beef shanks
1 onion, quartered
1 package soup greens (or 2 celery
    stalks, 1 carrot, 1 potato,
    1 turnip, and a sprig of parsley,
    all cleaned and chopped)

1 small bay leaf
2 whole peppercorns
1 clove
1½ teaspoons salt
6 cups water
1 celery root

¼ pound ham
2 ounces penne or elbow macaroni
3 tablespoons tomato paste
1 teaspoon dry chervil
4 tablespoons grated Parmesan
    cheese

In large Dutch oven combine beef shanks, onion, soup greens, bay leaf, peppercorns, clove, and salt. Add water; bring to boil. Skim any foam. Reduce heat to low; simmer covered 1½ to 2 hours. Remove meat; cool. Strain broth; skim fat. Return broth to pot.

Clean celery root, cut into thin sticks.

Dice meat from beef shanks.

Cut ham into thin strips.

Boil macaroni until tender in boiling salted water; drain.

Bring broth to boil.

Combine tomato paste with 1 cup broth; stir until dissolved. Add to broth in pot, along with celery root, diced beef, and ham. Cover; cook 15 minutes. Add macaroni and chervil; heat through. Sprinkle with Parmesan and serve.

roman-style vegetable soup

Yield: 4 generous servings

½ cup finely chopped salt pork
1 large onion, peeled, diced
1 clove garlic
3 carrots, peeled, diced
2 stalks celery, sliced
1 parsnip, peeled, diced
½ bunch parsley, chopped
2 large chopped tomatoes

1 quart beef broth
1 (16-ounce) can red kidney beans,
    drained
1 teaspoon crumbled sweet basil
Salt and pepper
1½ cups uncooked wide egg
    noodles
Grated Parmesan cheese

Render salt pork in large pan over moderate heat. Add onion and garlic; cook until tender. Add carrots, celery, parsnip, parsley, and tomatoes; stir well. Add beef broth, beans, basil, salt, and pepper. Bring to boil; reduce heat to low. Cover; cook 1 hour. Add noodles; simmer 15 minutes, until noodles are tender. Serve sprinkled with Parmesan cheese.

sicilian sausage soup

Yield: 4 servings

¼ pound sweet Italian sausage
    (with casing removed)
½ cup finely chopped onion
¼ cup chopped peeled carrots
¼ cup chopped celery
2 tablespoons chopped parsley
1 (16-ounce) can Italian-style peeled
    tomatoes, broken up with a fork

1 (13¾-ounce) can regular strength
    chicken broth
½ teaspoon crumbled dried sweet
    basil
¼ cup orzo (rice-shaped macaroni
    for soup, also called "soupettes")
Salt and pepper

In medium skillet, brown sausage; break it into small pieces as it cooks. Remove from skillet with a slotted spoon. Place into large saucepan.

Sauté onion in sausage drippings until tender. Remove onion with slotted spoon; add to sausage. Add vegetables, chicken broth, and basil to sausage mixture. Bring soup to boil; stir well. Cook over moderate heat 15 minutes. Stir in orzo and salt and pepper to taste. Reduce heat to low; simmer covered 20 minutes or until orzo is tender.

opposite: neapolitan minestrone

salads

cauliflower salad

Yield: 4 servings

1 small head cauliflower
¼ cup chopped red pepper or pimiento
2 tablespoons chopped fresh parsley (Italian flat
   leaf if available)
¼ cup sliced black olives

1 tablespoon chopped capers
1 tablespoon wine vinegar
3 tablespoons olive oil
½ teaspoon crumbled dried oregano

Wash and clean cauliflower; separate into florets. Slice florets into thick slices. Cook in boiling salted water until crisp but tender. Drain well. Gently mix cauliflower, pepper, parsley, olives, and capers in serving bowl.
   Combine vinegar, oil, and oregano; mix well. Pour over salad; refrigerate 1 hour before serving.
   This salad can be garnished with anchovies if you wish.

Note: Other cooked vegetables—for example, beets, broccoli, or green beans—can be substituted in this recipe.

green salad with croutons

Yield: 4 to 6 servings

croutons

2 tablespoons olive oil
1 clove garlic, peeled, sliced
1 cup cubed stale Italian bread with crust
   removed (save for bread crumbs)

salad dressing

½ cup olive oil
¼ cup red wine vinegar
½ teaspoon crumbled dried oregano
½ teaspoon salt
¼ teaspoon pepper

salad

1 medium head iceberg lettuce
1 medium head romaine lettuce
   or endive

¼ cup grated Parmesan cheese

Heat oil in small skillet. Sauté garlic in oil over moderate heat until lightly browned. Remove garlic with slotted spoon; discard. Add bread cubes; sauté, stirring frequently, until golden brown. Drain on paper towels.
   Combine dressing ingredients in a bottle or screw-top jar; shake well. Let stand at room temperature.
   Clean lettuce; pat dry. Tear into bite-size pieces; place in salad bowl. Refrigerate until serving time.
   To serve, sprinkle salad with cheese and croutons. Shake dressing well; pour over salad. Toss well; serve immediately.

macaroni salad with salami

Yield: 4 servings

1 cup cooked tubetti or other short macaroni
½ cup chopped green pepper
¼ cup chopped celery

½ cup cooked frozen peas, drained (undercook slightly
   so they retain their shape)
½ cup salami strips
2 sweet pickles, finely chopped

In mixing bowl lightly combine tubetti, pepper, celery, peas, salami, and pickles.

salad dressing

½ cup mayonnaise or salad dressing
3 tablespoons milk
1 tablespoon lemon juice
Salt, pepper, and cayenne

garnish

2 hard-cooked eggs, peeled, quartered
2 medium tomatoes, peeled, quartered
2 tablespoons chopped parsley

Combine mayonnaise, milk, and lemon juice in a small bowl. Season to taste with salt, pepper, and cayenne. Pour over salad; mix gently. Place in serving bowl; chill well.
   Garnish with eggs and tomatoes; sprinkle with parsley.

opposite: green salad with croutons

marinated vegetable salad

Yield: 6 servings

2 quarts water
2 teaspoons salt
1 (10-ounce) package Romano
   beans, partially defrosted
1 (10-ounce) package cauliflower

2 carrots, peeled, thinly sliced
1 medium zucchini, sliced ¼ inch
   thick
2 cloves garlic
1 teaspoon salt

¼ cup white wine vinegar
6 tablespoons olive oil
¼ teaspoon pepper
½ cup sliced ripe olives
1 medium onion, peeled, sliced,
   separated into rings

Combine water and salt in Dutch oven; bring to boil. Add beans, cauliflower, and carrots; cook 4 minutes. Add zucchini; cook 3 minutes. Drain in colander.

Peel garlic cloves; place on wooden board. Sprinkle with salt; mash well with side of knife. Combine garlic, vinegar, oil, and pepper in bottom of salad bowl; mix well. Add vegetables, olives, and onion; mix gently. Cover; refrigerate several hours or overnight before serving.

rice and chicken salad

This salad can be varied by substituting shrimp, lobster, cold beef, veal, or even salami for the chicken. In Italy it is served as either antipasto or as a light lunch.

Yield: 4 to 6 servings

1 cup rice, cooked al dente (firm to the bite)

dressing

1 teaspoon Dijon mustard
½ teaspoon salt
2 teaspoons red wine vinegar
6 tablespoons olive oil
½ cup finely diced Swiss cheese
¼ cup pitted, diced black olives

2 tablespoons pitted, diced green
   olives
¼ cup seeded, cored, diced sweet
   red or green pepper
3 tablespoons diced sour gherkins
1 whole chicken breast, boiled, diced

After the rice is cooked, rinse in cold water. Drain thoroughly; set aside.

In large salad bowl mix mustard, salt, and vinegar. Use a fork to blend and stir in the oil. Toss drained rice with dressing; coat well. Stir in remaining ingredients; mix gently. Serve salad cool, but not chilled.

mixed seafood salad

Yield: 4 servings

2 dozen mussels
2 dozen small clams
3 tablespoons olive oil
2 pounds small squid
½ cup white wine
1¼ pounds medium shrimp

dressing

4 tablespoons olive oil
2 tablespoons lemon juice
1 teaspoon Dijon mustard
Salt
Freshly ground pepper

garnish

2 tablespoons finely chopped
   parsley
Lettuce
Lemon wedges

Scrub mussels and clams well under cold running water.

Heat oil in large skillet with tight-fitting lid. Add mussels and clams; cover. Cook over medium-high heat, shaking pan occasionally, until shellfish open (approximately 10 minutes). Remove clams and mussels from shells; cool. Reserve juices; strain through sieve.

Wash squid; remove tentacles. Remove head, chitinous pen, and viscera; wash mantle well.

In large saucepan combine wine and reserved juices from shellfish. Bring to boil over moderate heat. Add squid body and tentacles; cover. Simmer 10 minutes. Add shrimp; cook 15 minutes. (Squid should be tender and shrimp cooked through and pink.) Drain well. Shell shrimp; slice squid body into thin rings.

In large bowl combine clams, mussels, squid, and shrimp.

Combine dressing ingredients.

Pour dressing over seafood; mix well. Sprinkle with parsley; marinate in refrigerator 2 hours.

Serve on beds of lettuce; garnish with lemon wedges.

opposite: rice and chicken salad

pasta, rice, and grain

cannelloni

Yield: 4 or 5 servings

pasta

15 (4½ × 5-inch) paper-thin pieces
   fresh pasta dough or 15 entrée
   crepes

Cook pasta, if used, in large amount of boiling salted water 5 minutes, until just tender. Drain well; place on paper towels to dry.

cannelloni sauce

1 large onion, peeled
2 cloves, garlic, peeled, minced
2 ounces slab bacon
2 cups Italian-style plum tomatoes
   (undrained)
¼ pound mushrooms, sliced
3 tablespoons tomato paste
3 tablespoons red wine
Salt and pepper

Begin sauce while noodles cook. Finely mince onion, garlic, and bacon together. Transfer mixture to heavy skillet; sauté over moderate heat until mixture begins to brown. Add tomatoes; break up with fork. Add remaining sauce ingredients; stir well. Cover; simmer 20 minutes.

cannelloni filling

2 tablespoons olive oil
1 large onion, peeled, chopped
1 clove garlic, peeled, finely minced
1 pound lean ground beef
2 chicken livers
1 (10-ounce) package frozen
   chopped|spinach, defrosted
2 eggs, beaten
½ cup freshly grated Parmesan
   cheese
½ teaspoon crumbled oregano
Salt and pepper

Heat oil in large skillet. Add onion and garlic; sauté until tender. Add ground beef; sauté, breaking up into small pieces, 5 minutes. Add livers; cook until meat is browned. Remove livers; finely chop. Drain meat mixture. Combine meat and livers in large mixing bowl.
Place spinach in sieve; press dry with back of spoon. Add to meat mixture along with remaining filling ingredients; mix well.

garnish

¼ cup grated Parmesan cheese
2 tablespoons melted butter

Place 3 tablespoons filling on each pasta rectangle or crepe; roll up jelly-roll fashion.
Pour thin layer of sauce in bottom of shallow casserole dish. Place pasta rolls close together in dish. Cover with remaining sauce. Garnish with cheese; drizzle with butter. Bake at 350°F 30 minutes.

opposite: cannelloni

egg noodles

Yield: About ¾ pound

1⅓ cups flour
½ teaspoon salt
2 eggs

2 teaspoons olive oil
2 teaspoons water

Combine flour and salt in mixing bowl. Make a well in center.

Beat eggs, oil, and water together; pour into well. Mix thoroughly; add a little more water if necessary to form a stiff dough. Turn out onto lightly floured surface. Knead to form smooth, elastic dough (about 15 minutes). Let rest, covered, 30 minutes.

To roll by hand: Divide dough into four equal parts. Lightly flour a smooth surface. Roll dough ¼ at a time until it is as thin as you can roll it. Ideally it should be 1/16 inch thick. Select a ball-bearing rolling pin if possible, since it is very easy to get blisters. Cut according to recipe of your choice, or use the following to substitute for package noodles.

Tagliatelle: Roll up like a scroll; cut into 3/8-inch strips. Unroll; dry on a towel.

Lasagna: Cut into strips 2 inches wide and as long as your baking dish; dry on towels.

Manicotti: Cut into squares 5 × 5 inches; dry on towels.

To roll by pasta machine: If you enjoy homemade noodles and pasta and make them frequently, a pasta machine might be a good investment. It consists of 2 rollers that can be moved close together or far apart and turned by a crank. Several cutting blades are provided. The machine can also be used to roll wonton wrappers or certain specialty breads such as poppadums. It is not necessary to knead the dough by hand if you are rolling it by machine as both operations can be accomplished at the same time.

Let dough rest without kneading; divide into quarters. Take dough, one-quarter at a time, and pass through machine with rollers set as far apart as possible (usually number 10 or highest numerical setting on machine). Fold dough into thirds; pass through again. After passing dough through machine 10 times, turn setting down one notch; roll through. Continue to roll dough, reducing setting one notch each time, until desired thickness is achieved. The dough strip will become long. Do not fold it. If it becomes unwieldy, cut it in half and roll pieces separately. Roll to slightly less than 1/16th inch thick. Cut as directed above; dry.

Noodles can be prepared ahead. Simply roll them, cut, and dry for ½ hour, then freeze. It is best to quick-freeze noodles on a tray, then carefully transfer them to a bag or box; seal. Remove from freezer when ready to use. Cook same as freshly made pasta.

To cook, bring 4 to 5 quarts salted water to boil. Float 1 tablespoon oil on surface of water. Add pasta a few pieces at a time; stir. Cook until pasta floats to surface of water. Test for doneness. It should be firm, not mushy. Drain well.

Yield for these pasta recipes is based on machine-rolled pasta. If you are rolling the dough by hand, make twice the amount of dough, since the product will not be as thin. If you have extra, make noodles and freeze them for future use.

Green Noodles: Omit water. Add ¼ cup well-drained, cooked, pureed spinach. Proceed as above.

fettuccine with zucchini and mushrooms

Yield: 4 main-dish servings; 6 servings as a pasta course.

zucchini and mushroom sauce

½ pound mushrooms
1¼ pounds young zucchini squash
¾ cup (1½ sticks) butter
1 cup heavy cream

fettuccine

1 pound fettuccine noodles
Boiling salted water
1 tablespoon olive oil
¾ cup freshly grated Parmesan cheese

½ cup chopped parsley
(preferably Italian flat-leaf)
Salt and white pepper
Freshly grated Parmesan cheese

Wipe mushrooms with damp cloth, or wash if much dirt is adhering to them; pat dry with paper towels. Trim as necessary; slice.

Scrub zucchini; slice into julienne strips.

Melt ¼ cup (½ stick) butter in large heavy skillet over moderate heat. Add mushrooms; saute 4 minutes. Add zucchini; sauté 3 minutes. Add cream and remaining butter, cut into small pieces. Reduce heat to low. Heat through, stirring gently.

Cook noodles in large amount of boiling salted water with oil floating on surface. Consult package directions for cooking times, but test frequently so noodles are *al dente*. Drain well. Place noodles in warm bowl. Add ¾ cup Parmesan, and parsley; toss lightly. Add sauce, salt, and pepper; lightly toss with 2 forks. Place on warm platter; serve with freshly grated Parmesan.

opposite: egg noodles

lasagna

Yield: 6 servings

pasta

3 quarts water

2 teaspoons salt

1 tablespoon vegetable oil

8 ounces lasagna noodles

Combine water and salt in large kettle. Float oil on surface of water. Bring to boil. Slowly add lasagna noodles, a few at a time. Cook 15 minutes. Drain; rinse with cold water.

lasagna sauce

1 pound ground beef

2 mild Italian sausage links
   (casing removed)

1 tablespoon olive oil

1 medium onion, finely diced

1 clove garlic, minced

1 (28-ounce) can peeled Italian
   tomatoes

1 (6-ounce) can tomato paste

½ teaspoon crumbled dried
   oregano

½ teaspoon crumbled dried sweet
   basil

1 teaspoon sugar

lasagna filling

8 ounces ricotta or pot cheese

8 ounces mozzarella cheese,
   thinly sliced

½ cup freshly grated Parmesan
   cheese

Meanwhile, brown ground beef and sausages in large skillet. Remove from pan; pour off drippings. Add oil to skillet. Sauté onion and garlic over low heat 5 minutes. Add tomatoes, broken up with a fork, tomato paste, and seasonings. Stir well. Add meat to sauce. Cook over low heat 40 minutes or until thick.

Lightly grease 13 X 9 X 2-inch baking dish. Ladle approximately ¾ cup sauce into pan. Top with ⅓ of noodles. Dot with ½ of ricotta and ½ of mozzarella. Add a layer of sauce, ⅓ of noodles, and remaining ricotta and mozzarella. Top with more sauce, then with remaining noodles. Top with remaining sauce and sprinkle with Parmesan. Bake at 350°F 30 minutes or until heated through. Serve with garlic bread and green salad.

linguine with salmon sauce

Yield: 4 servings

2 cloves garlic, minced

¼ cup butter

¼ cup olive oil

1 teaspoon coarsely cracked pepper

1 (7¾-ounce) can salmon

Clam juice

1 pound linguine or thin spaghetti, cooked

2 tablespoons chopped parsley

Sauté garlic in butter and oil until lightly browned. Add pepper.

Drain liquid from salmon into measuring cup; add clam juice to make 1 cup. Flake salmon; add with liquid to garlic mixture. Bring to simmer. Just before serving over linguine, stir in parsley.

macaroni with sauce amatrice

Yield: 4 servings

sauce amatrice

2 tablespoons olive oil

2 cloves garlic, peeled, minced

¼ pound salt pork, diced

1 small onion, chopped

¼ cup dry white wine

1 (28-ounce) can Italian plum
   tomatoes, drained, minced

1 teaspoon sugar

1 teaspoon chili powder

½ teaspoon paprika

½ teaspoon crumbled dried sweet
   basil

½ teaspoon crumbled dried
   oregano

Salt and pepper

Heat oil in large saucepan. Add garlic, salt pork, and onion. Sauté until onion is tender. Add wine; cook until it has evaporated. Add tomatoes and spices. Simmer 20 minutes, uncovered.

pasta

3 quarts water

1 tablespoon salt

1 tablespoon cooking oil

12 ounces penne or other macaroni

Grated Parmesan cheese

Meanwhile, heat water to boiling. Add salt. Float oil on surface of water. Add penne; cook until *al dente*. Drain. Place in serving bowl; top with sauce. Serve with Parmesan cheese.

opposite: linguine with salmon sauce

manicotti

This recipe only looks long! Really, stuffed manicotti are quite easy to prepare and offer a great deal of variety. These noodles can be prepared ahead and baked just before serving. In using this recipe, select the noodle or substitute of your choice and select *one* of the fillings. Top with the sauce, and bake.

Yield: 6 servings

pasta

12 packaged manicotti shells
Boiling water
or 12 prepared entrée crepes

or 12 cooked homemade manicotti
noodles, 6 inches square
(see Index for Egg Noodles)

If using manicotti shells, cover with boiling water; let stand 5 minutes. (Of course you can cook manicotti noodles in boiling salted water before stuffing, but it really isn't necessary, and they break very easily when cooked and stuffed). Drain; rinse in cold water. Set aside while making the filling of your choice.

manicotti filling 1

1 pound ricotta or pot cheese
1 cup grated mozzarella cheese
   (¼ pound)
¼ cup grated Parmesan cheese
1 tablespoon dehydrated parsley
   flakes
1 egg, lightly beaten
½ teaspoon salt
¼ teaspoon white pepper
¼ teaspoon garlic powder

manicotti filling II

1 pound ricotta or pot cheese
¼ cup grated Parmesan cheese
1 tablespoon dehydrated parsley
   flakes
3 links Italian sweet sausage,
   removed from casing, cooked,
   chopped
1 egg, lightly beaten
¼ teaspoon salt
1/8 teaspoon pepper

Combine all ingredients and mix well for both fillings.

manicotti filling III

1 medium onion, minced
1 clove garlic, peeled, chopped
2 tablespoons butter or margarine
1 (10-ounce) package frozen chopped spinach,
   thawed and pressed dry in a sieve

½ cup finely chopped chicken
1 teaspoon lemon juice
½ teaspoon salt

¼ teaspoon ground nutmeg
1 pound ricotta cheese
1 egg, lightly beaten

Sauté onion and garlic in butter until transparent. Add remaining ingredients; mix well.

manicotti filling IV

2 tablespoons olive oil
1 small onion, chopped
½ pound ground beef
¼ pound Italian sweet sausage
¼ cup marinara sauce

¼ cup Italian-style bread crumbs
1 cup grated mozzarella cheese (¼ pound)
½ tablespoon dehydrated
   chopped parsley flakes
Salt and pepper

Heat oil in medium skillet. Add onion, beef, and sausage. Cook over moderate heat until meat is lightly browned. Stir frequently; break meat into small pieces. Drain well; remove from heat. Let cool 5 minutes. Add remaining ingredients; mix well.

sauce

3 cups marinara sauce
½ cup water (omit water if using
   crepes or homemade noodles)

3 tablespoons grated Parmesan
   cheese

Combine marinara sauce and water in medium saucepan. Heat on low while stuffing noodles.
Stuff each shell or pancake with ⅓ to ½ cup filling. Pour ¾ cup of heated sauce into 13 × 9 × 2-inch baking dish; tilt to coat lightly. Place stuffed noodles in dish. Top with remaining sauce. If using the manicotti noodles, cover with foil; bake 45 minutes at 375°F. Uncover; sprinkle with Parmesan. Bake 5 minutes. If using crepes or homemade noodles, bake at 350°F 30 minutes, uncovered. Sprinkle with grated Parmesan. Bake 5 minutes.
Serve with a green salad and garlic bread.

opposite: manicotti

manicotti venetian-style

Yield: 6 to 8 servings

| 1 (8-ounce) package manicotti noodles | Boiling salted water | 1 tablespoon cooking oil |

Cook manicotti shells in large pan of boiling salted water, with oil floating on surface, 15 minutes, until *al dente*. Drain well; rinse with cold water. Set aside.

meat filling

1 pound meat-loaf mixture (ground pork, beef, and veal)	1 clove garlic, peeled, minced	¼ cup finely chopped parsley
1 large onion, peeled, diced	1 egg, well-beaten	1 teaspoon crumbled sweet basil
	1 cup fresh bread crumbs	Salt and Pepper

In heavy skillet cook meat-loaf mixture, onion, and garlic over low heat until meat loses all red color. Break meat into small chunks as it cooks. Drain well. Combine meat mixture, egg, bread crumbs, parsley, and seasonings; mix well.

Stuff manicotti shells with filling. Place in lightly greased baking dish.

manicotti sauce

6 tablespoons butter	White pepper	1 cup light cream	Nutmeg
6 tablespoons flour	¼ teaspoon ground nutmeg	¾ cup freshly grated Parmesan cheese	Chopped parsley
½ teaspoon salt	1½ cups chicken broth		

Melt butter in large saucepan. Add flour; cook, stirring constantly, until bubbly. Add seasonings; stir well. Add broth and cream all at once. Cook, stirring constantly, until thickened. Remove from heat; stir in cheese.

Pour sauce evenly over stuffed manicotti noodles. Sprinkle lightly with nutmeg and chopped parsley. Bake at 350°F 30 minutes. Serve immediately.

pasta (agnolotti) with cream sauce

Yield: 6 servings; about 80 agnolotti

pasta dough	pasta filling		cream sauce
2 cups all-purpose flour	2 tablespoons olive oil	1/8 pound finely chopped prosciutto	3 tablespoons butter
1 teaspoon salt	¼ cup finely chopped onion	¼ teaspoon crushed rosemary	6 tablespoons flour
3 eggs		1/8 teaspoon nutmeg	Salt and pepper
2 teaspoons olive oil	¼ pound ground veal	Salt and pepper	1½ cups chicken broth
1 tablespoon water	1 egg		1½ cups light cream
	1 cup cooked finely chopped chicken breast		½ cup freshly grated Parmesan cheese
			1/8 teaspoon ground nutmeg

Prepare pasta dough. Combine flour and salt in mixing bowl.

Combine eggs, oil, and water; mix well. Add to flour; mix to form stiff dough. Turn out onto board; knead 5 minutes. Cover with plastic wrap; let rest 30 minutes.

Prepare filling while dough rests. Heat oil in small, heavy skillet. Add onion; sauté until tender. Add veal; cook, stirring, until meat is crumbly and lightly browned. Transfer mixture to mixing bowl; cool slightly. Add remaining filling ingredients; mix well.

Divide pasta dough into 4 parts. Cover any dough not being used, to prevent drying. Roll dough, one part at a time, on lightly floured surface to 1/16 inch thick. Cut into 3-inch circles with round cutter or glass. Reroll scraps. Place heaping ½ teaspoon filling on each round. Dampen edge of circle with a little water. Fold into half-moon shape; seal. With folded edge toward you, bring two ends together; pinch. (Finished pasta looks like small circular hats with cuffs.) Place pasta on tray; cover with towel until ready to cook, or freeze for future use.

Prepare sauce. Melt butter in medium saucepan. Add flour, salt, and pepper; mix well. Cook 1 minute. Gradually stir in broth. Cook, stirring constantly, until thickened; remove from heat. Stir in cream. Return to heat; cook, stirring constantly, until thickened. Add cheese and nutmeg. Keep sauce warm while cooking pasta.

Cook pasta 10 minutes in large amount boiling salted water, with small amount oil added. Drain well. Serve immediately, topped with cream sauce. Sprinkle with additional Parmesan, if desired. Agnolotti can also be served with marinara sauce.

Note: If available, use pasta machine for rolling dough.

opposite: pasta with cream sauce

ravioli

Yield: About 96 ravioli; 6 to 8 servings

pasta

1 double recipe Egg Noodles
(see Index)

ravioli filling

¾ pound meat-loaf mix
¼ cup dry bread crumbs
2 tablespoons grated Parmesan
cheese
1 egg
1 tablespoon dehydrated parsley
flakes
½ teaspoon garlic salt
¼ teaspoon pepper

cornmeal
4 quarts boiling water
1 tablespoon salt
1 tablespoon cooking oil

Prepare the pasta according to the recipe; let rest, covered, 15 minutes.

Combine filling ingredients in a bowl; mix well. Refrigerate until ready to use.

Divide dough into 8 pieces. Roll 1 piece at a time on lightly floured surface. Keep remainder of dough tightly covered. Roll dough as thin as possible. If using a pasta machine to roll dough, roll it to slightly less than 1/16th inch thick. Cut dough into 2-inch squares. Place 1 teaspoon of filling in center of ½ of squares. Top with remainder of squares. Press edges together tightly to seal. Moisten edges with a little water if necessary to ensure a tight seal. Dust cookie sheet lightly with cornmeal. Place ravioli on sheet. Refrigerate, covered, or freeze until ready to cook.

To cook, heat 4 quarts of water to boiling. Add salt, and float oil on surface of water. Drop ravioli into water a few at a time; Stir to prevent them from sticking to bottom of pan. Reduce heat so that water boils gently. Cook approximately 12 minutes, until tender; drain.

Serve hot with your favorite tomato or meat sauce and grated cheese, or toss with melted butter and freshly grated Parmesan cheese.

Note: Any leftover filling can be fried and added to the meat sauce for the ravioli. Any of the other fillings used in this section for manicotti or tortellini can be used instead of the meat filling given here.

rice milanese-style

Yield: 4 servings

½ small onion, finely minced
½ cup long-grain white rice
1 tablespoon butter
1 tablespoon olive oil

2 teaspoons beef marrow
2 tablespoons dry white wine
Pinch of saffron
2 cups hot beef broth

1 tablespoon butter
2 tablespoons grated Parmesan
cheese

Sauté onion and rice in 1 tablespoon butter and oil over moderate heat until very lightly browned. Add beef marrow; cook gently until it melts. Add wine; cook until it is absorbed.

Dissolve saffron in hot beef broth. Add beef broth a little at a time. Continue to cook, stirring constantly, until all liquid is absorbed and rice is tender and creamy in consistency, 18 to 20 minutes. Stir in remaining butter and cheese; let cheese melt. Serve immediately. Rice does not reheat well.

risotto

Risotto is not simply rice cooked in chicken broth. The gradual addition of the liquid, a little at a time until the grain has absorbed it, allows the final dish to be creamy and together but not dry or runny.

Yield: 4 servings

4 tablespoons butter
1 cup medium-grain or short-grain
rice (preferably Italian)

4 tablespoons finely minced onion
2 tablespoons dry white wine
Pinch of saffron

4 cups hot chicken broth
2 tablespoons grated Parmesan
cheese

Melt 3 tablespoons butter in heavy saucepan. Add rice and onion; sauté until lightly browned, stirring constantly. Add wine; cook until absorbed.

Dissolve saffron in chicken broth. Add broth to rice a little at a time; continue cooking, stirring constantly, until all liquid is absorbed and rice is tender and creamy in consistency. (This should take 18 to 20 minutes.) Add remaining butter and cheese; mix well. Let cheese melt. Serve immediately.

opposite: ravioli

venetian rice and peas

Yield: 4 to 6 servings

3 tablespoons butter or margarine
¼ cup chopped onion
2 cups regular-strength chicken broth

1 cup raw long-grain rice
1 (10-ounce) package frozen green peas
½ cup diced cooked ham

Salt and pepper
Grated Parmesan cheese

Melt butter in large saucepan. Sauté onion until transparent.

Meanwhile, heat chicken broth to boiling.

Add rice to onions; stir to coat with butter. Add peas, ham, and chicken broth; stir well. Cover; cook over low heat approximately 20 minutes, until all liquid is absorbed. Sprinkle with Parmesan cheese and serve.

rigatoni, stuffed

Cook a pound of rigatoni to be sure you have enough, since they break very easily. Eat any leftover unstuffed rigatoni with marinara sauce.

Yield: 8 servings

rigatoni sauce

4 tablespoons olive oil
2 pounds meat-loaf mixture (ground beef, veal, and pork)
4 cloves garlic, peeled, chopped
½ cup finely chopped celery
½ cup finely chopped carrots

½ cup finely chopped green pepper
¼ cup finely chopped parsley
1 medium onion, finely chopped
1 (6-ounce) can tomato paste
¾ cup water

1 (28-ounce) can peeled Italian tomatoes
2 teaspoons sugar
1 teaspoon salt
½ teaspoon pepper
½ teaspoon crumbled dried sweet basil
½ teaspoon crumbled dried oregano

Heat 2 tablespoons oil in heavy skillet. Add meat and 3 cloves garlic. Sauté slowly, without browning, until meat loses it pink color. Drain; reserve ½ of meat mixture for pasta stuffing.

In Dutch oven, heat rest of oil and sauté celery, carrots, green pepper, parsley, onion, and 1 clove garlic over medium heat until limp. Add tomato paste and water.

Sieve tomatoes or puree in blender; add to sauce. Add ½ of cooked meat, and seasonings. Bring to boil. Reduce heat to low; simmer 1½ to 2 hours.

pasta and filling

1 tablespoon cooking oil
1 pound rigatoni No. 28
2 (10-ounce) packages frozen chopped spinach, thawed

¼ cup grated Parmesan cheese
½ cup plain dry bread crumbs
2 eggs

Salt and pepper
1 clove garlic, peeled, minced
topping
½ cup grated Parmesan cheese

Meanwhile, prepare and stuff pasta. In large kettle, bring 4½ quarts salted water to boil over high heat. Float oil on surface of water. Add rigatoni; stir well. Reduce heat to medium-high. Cook, stirring occasionally, approximately 12 minutes, until almost done. Drain well; rinse with cold water.

Squeeze spinach in a sieve until dry. Combine spinach, cheese, remaining meat, bread crumbs, eggs, salt, pepper, and garlic; mix well. Stuff rigatoni with mixture; use pastry tube or fingers.

Lightly grease a 13 X 9 X 2-inch baking dish. Layer rigatoni and sauce in baking dish. Sprinkle with ½ cup Parmesan cheese. Bake at 350°F 30 to 45 minutes or until hot and bubbly.

Note: This casserole can be prepared in advance and refrigerated until baking time. Make it a day ahead if you are serving it for a party.

semolina dumplings roman-style

Yield: 3 or 4 servings

2 cups milk
1 tablespoon butter
½ teaspoon salt
Pinch of freshly grated nutmeg

Ground white pepper to taste
½ cup semolina or farina
2 eggs, beaten
½ cup grated Parmesan cheese

for garnish

2 tablespoons melted butter
1 tablespoon grated Parmesan cheese

Butter a cookie sheet; set aside.

In a heavy saucepan combine milk, butter, salt, nutmeg, and pepper. Bring to boil over moderate heat. Slowly add semolina, stirring constantly. Reduce heat to low; cook until very thick and a spoon will stand unsupported in center of pan. Remove from heat. Add eggs and ½ cup cheese; mix well. Spread on cookie sheet in a rectangle ½ inch thick. Refrigerate until firm.

Cut into rounds about 1½ inches in diameter (or cut into squares or triangles, if you prefer). Arrange in greased casserole or baking dish, slightly overlapping. Drizzle with melted butter. Sprinkle with Parmesan.   Bake in preheated 350°F oven 20 minutes. Serve hot.

opposite: venetian rice with peas

jumbo shells, stuffed

Yield: 4 servings

16 jumbo shells (6 ounces)

2 tablespoons olive oil
½ cup finely chopped onion
1 clove garlic, peeled, minced

1 (16-ounce) can peeled Italian
  tomatoes, pureed
3 tablespoons tomato paste

½ teaspoon sugar
½ teaspoon mixed Italian seasoning
Salt and pepper

filling

1 (10½-ounce) package frozen
  spinach
1 (16-ounce) package ricotta

1 egg, slightly beaten
¼ teaspoon ground nutmeg
Salt and pepper

½ cup freshly grated Parmesan
  cheese

Cook shells, according to package directions, in large amount boiling salted water until *al dente*. Drain; rinse with cold water. Set aside.

Meanwhile, make sauce. Heat oil in medium saucepan. Add onion and garlic; sauté until tender. Add remaining sauce ingredients; mix well. Bring to boil. Reduce heat to low; simmer ½ hour.

Place spinach in sieve; press dry. In mixing bowl combine ricotta, egg, spinach, and seasonings; mix well.

Stuff filling into cooked shells. Place side by side in lightly greased 9 × 9-inch pan. Pour sauce over shells. Sprinkle with cheese. Bake in preheated 350°F oven 30 minutes. Serve with garlic bread and green salad.

spaghetti with sauce and meatballs

Yield: 4 servings

meatballs

1 pound lean ground beef
½ cup Italian-style bread crumbs
1 egg, slightly beaten
1 tablespoon dried onion flakes
Salt and pepper
3 tablespoons cooking oil

Combine beef, bread crumbs, egg, onion flakes, salt, and pepper; mix well. Form into meatballs the size of a walnut. Brown in medium-size skillet in cooking oil; drain.

tomato sauce

2 tablespoons olive oil
1 medium onion, chopped
1 clove garlic, minced
1 (28-ounce) can Italian-style peeled
  tomatoes
1 (6-ounce) can tomato paste
¾ cup water (or refill tomato-paste can)
1½ teaspoons mixed Italian herbs
1 teaspoon sugar
½ cup dry red wine

plus one of the following:

½ pound stewing beef, cut into
  1½-inch cubes and browned in oil
or
1½ cups leftover cooked pork
  roast, cut into 1½-inch cubes
or
1 (4-ounce) can sliced mushrooms,
  drained

Heat oil in large saucepan. Add onion and garlic; sauté 5 minutes.

Puree tomatoes in blender or force through a sieve. Add to onion mixture, with tomato paste, water, seasonings, and wine. Bring to boil; reduce heat to low. Add meatballs and 1 or more items from *plus section*. Simmer covered 1 to 1½ hours or until thick.

spaghetti

4½ quarts boiling salted water
1 tablespoon cooking oil
12 ounces thin spaghetti

Bring salted water to boil. Float oil on surface of water. Add spaghetti; stir with fork to prevent sticking. Cook according to package directions; drain.

To serve in the Italian manner, separate meat from sauce. Toss sauce and spaghetti together to coat lightly. Serve meat on a platter so guests can serve themselves. Pass grated Parmesan cheese.

opposite: spaghetti with sauce and meatballs

poultry

breast of chicken with italian ham

Yield: 4 servings

4 individual chicken breasts (about ½ pound each), skinned, boned
Salt and pepper
1 teaspoon crumbled dried leaf sage
¼ pound prosciutto, thinly sliced
4 tablespoons butter

1 small onion, minced
1 clove garlic, minced
½ pound mushrooms, cleaned, sliced
¼ cup chicken broth
¼ cup white wine
2 tablespoons chopped fresh parsley

Place chicken between sheets of waxed paper; pound with flat side of cleaver or bottom of heavy bottle to form cutlets of even thickness. Remove waxed paper. Season with salt and pepper. Sprinkle with sage. Evenly distribute ham atop chicken. Fold in half; secure with toothpick.

Melt butter in heavy skillet. Add chicken; cook over moderate heat, turning until lightly browned. Remove from pan.

Add onion and garlic to pan; cook 1 minute. Add mushrooms; cook until mushroom liquid evaporates. Return chicken to skillet; spoon mushrooms over them. Add chicken broth and wine; cover. Simmer 20 minutes. Transfer to platter; cover chicken with mushrooms. Pour over pan juices; sprinkle with parsley.

capellini and chicken

Yield: 4 to 6 servings

1 large chicken (about 4 pounds), roasted
10 tablespoons butter
½ pound mushrooms, sliced
½ cup flour
4 cups chicken broth

1½ cups milk
½ cup heavy cream
Salt and pepper
1 pound capellini
½ cup bread crumbs
½ cup grated Asiago cheese

Separate meat from chicken bones; discard bones. Dice chicken into cubes. Set aside.
Heat 2 tablespoons butter; sauté mushrooms 5 minutes.
Melt remaining butter in another pan; blend in flour, broth, and milk. Stir constantly over low heat; cook until sauce begins to thicken. Add cream, and salt and pepper to taste.
Cook capellini *al dente*, no longer than 4 minutes; drain. Place in well-greased casserole. Cover with chicken and mushrooms; pour sauce over all. Sprinkle top with bread crumbs and cheese. Bake at 450°F about 30 minutes, or until bread crumbs are browned and the sauce bubbles.

chicken cacciatore

Yield: 4 servings

1 (3-pound) chicken
3 tablespoons vegetable oil
1 clove garlic
½ teaspoon salt
¼ teaspoon pepper
1 teaspoon rosemary

6 anchovy fillets, chopped
⅓ cup wine vinegar
1⅓ cups dry red wine
3 tablespoons tomato paste
½ cup chicken bouillon

Cut chicken into serving pieces.
Heat oil in large frypan; sauté chicken and garlic 5 minutes. Turn chicken often. Remove garlic. Add salt, pepper, rosemary, anchovies, vinegar, and wine. Simmer, uncovered, until liquid is reduced by one-third.
Dissolve tomato paste in bouillon; pour over chicken. Simmer, covered, 20 minutes or until chicken is done.

opposite: breast of chicken with Italian ham

chicken florence-style

Yield: 4 servings

1 (2½- to 3-pound) chicken
2 tablespoons olive oil
1 medium onion, chopped
1 clove garlic, minced
4 large fresh tomatoes, peeled,
  chopped (canned tomatoes can be
  substituted if drained and chopped)

4 large green olives, chopped
½ teaspoon crumbled dried sweet
  basil
½ teaspoon crumbled dried oregano
½ teaspoon celery salt
¼ teaspoon pepper
4 bay leaves

Wash chicken. Drain; pat dry. Cut chicken into quarters.

Cut 4 (10-inch) pieces aluminum foil; grease with olive oil. Place a piece of chicken in center of each piece of foil.

Combine onion, garlic, tomatoes, olives, basil, oregano, celery salt, and pepper; mix well. Spoon some over each piece of chicken. Add 1 bay leaf to each package. Place on cookie sheet. Bake at 425°F 40 minutes. Serve from packages, with a green salad and garlic bread.

chicken hunter's-style

Yield: 4 servings

1 (2½-pound) frying chicken, cut up
½ cup flour
Salt and pepper
⅓ cup olive oil
1 medium onion, peeled, sliced
1 green pepper, cleaned, sliced lengthwise
1 clove garlic, minced
1 (16-ounce) can plum tomatoes
¼ cup dry white wine
½ pound mushrooms, cleaned, sliced

Wash chicken well; pat dry.

Combine flour, salt, and pepper. Dredge chicken well.

Heat oil in large skillet. Add chicken; brown well on all sides. Remove from pan. Add onion, green pepper, and garlic; sauté until tender. Drain off fat remaining in pan.

Break tomatoes into pieces with fork; add to skillet. Add wine; stir well. Bring mixture to boil over moderate heat. Add chicken; cover. Reduce heat; simmer 45 minutes. Add mushrooms; cook 15 to 20 minutes, until chicken and mushrooms are tender.

chicken marinara

This makes a great picnic dish.

Yield: 4 servings

½ cup all-purpose flour
1 teaspoon salt
¼ teaspoon pepper
1 (2½- to 3-pound) broiler-fryer
  chicken, cut-up
3 tablespoons butter or margarine

1 (15½-ounce) can marinara
  sauce or 2 cups homemade
  marinara sauce
1 teaspoon dried dillweed
2 tablespoons grated Parmesan
  cheese

Combine the four, salt, and pepper in brown paper bag. Add chicken a few pieces at a time; shake until coated with flour mixture. Place chicken in single layer in shallow baking dish. Dot with butter. Bake at 450°F 25 minutes. Remove from oven. Pour sauce over chicken. Sprinkle with dillweed and cheese. Reduce heat to 350°F; bake 25 minutes. Serve hot or cold.

opposite: chicken marinara

chicken parmesan with mushroom marsala sauce

Yield: 6 servings

2 to 3 tablespoons olive oil
6 to 8 pats butter
1 cup seasoned bread crumbs
1 cup freshly grated Parmesan cheese

1 tablespoon Herbes d'Provence (or herbs of your choice)
6 single chicken breasts (deboned)

1 cup flour seasoned with salt and pepper, on plate
2 eggs, beaten in medium-size bowl

Pour oil in center of 12-inch frying pan. Place pats of butter around oil; heat slowly to cooking temperature. Combine bread crumbs, cheese, and herbs on plate.

Wash and pat dry chicken. Coat with seasoned flour; dip in eggs. Coat with bread-crumb mixture. Set aside on waxed paper or rack; repeat procedure for all pieces. Let stand in refrigerator 2 to 3 hours. Place all pieces in frying pan at same time; fry to golden brown. Pour sauce over chicken just before serving.

mushroom marsala sauce

1 pound fresh mushrooms
3 to 4 tablespoons butter
⅓ cup marsala wine (or to taste)

Clean mushrooms; sauté in butter. Add wine; stir until hot (do not bring to boil).

chicken shoemaker's-style

Yield: 4 servings

1 (2½- to 3-pound) frying chicken
2 tablespoons olive oil
3 tablespoons butter
Salt and pepper
1 clove garlic, minced

2 tablespoons chopped green onions
1 cup sliced fresh mushrooms
½ teaspoon crumbled dried tarragon

½ cup chicken broth
½ cup dry white wine
¼ pound chicken livers
1 tablespoon chopped parsley

Cut up chicken, bones and all. Cut into quarters. Remove legs, thighs, and wings. Cut each quarter into 3 or 4 parts. Cut each wing or thigh in half. Wash chicken; pat dry.

Heat oil and 2 tablespoons butter in large skillet over moderate heat. Add chicken; sauté until browned. Season with salt and pepper. Remove from pan.

Sauté garlic, onions, and mushrooms until tender. Add tarragon, broth, wine, and browned chicken pieces. Bring to boil; reduce heat to low. Cover; cook 30 minutes.

Melt remaining butter in small skillet. Sauté livers 5 minutes, until almost cooked through. Add to chicken; simmer 5 minutes.

Garnish with parsley; serve.

chicken tetrazzini

Yield: 4 to 6 servings

1 stewing chicken, about 3 to 4 pounds
2 onions
2 carrots
Parsley, thyme, and 1 bay leaf
½ pound spaghetti

6 tablespoons butter
Dash of garlic powder
4 tablespoons flour
½ cup white wine
Salt and pepper

6 to 8 mushrooms, sliced
3 to 4 tablespoons whipping cream
¼ cup grated Parmesan cheese
2 tablespoons dried bread crumbs
2 tablespoons sliced almonds, browned

Preheat oven to 400°F.

Cook chicken slowly in water with onions, carrots, and herbs until tender. Let cool in stock, if possible overnight. Remove skin and bones; cook them in stock until well-flavored and reduced to 2 to 3 cups.

Boil spaghetti in usual way; finish in 1 tablespoon butter flavored with a little garlic powder. Place in fireproof dish; keep warm.

Make velouté sauce: Melt 4 tablespoons butter; add flour. When blended, add 1½ cups chicken stock. Bring to boil; cook 2 minutes. Add wine; simmer few minutes.

Meanwhile, cut cold chicken into long strips. Place in mound on spaghetti; sprinkle with salt and pepper.

Cook mushrooms in 1 tablespoon butter 2 or 3 minutes; put on chicken.

Add cream to sauce; check seasoning. Spoon sauce over dish; sprinkle top with cheese and crumbs. Bake in oven 10 to 15 minutes, until well-heated and top is brown and crisp. Sprinkle almonds over top. Serve at once.

opposite: chicken tetrazzini

chicken with garlic and oil

Yield: 4 servings

1 (2½- to 3-pound) frying chicken, cut-up
½ cup olive oil
4 medium potatoes
6 medium carrots

1 medium onion
2 cloves garlic, peeled, chopped
Juice of 1 lemon
Salt and freshly ground black pepper

Wash chicken well; pat dry.

Pour oil into bottom of 14 × 10 × 2½-inch pan or other large roasting pan. Dip chicken pieces into oil; turn to coat. Turn chicken skin-side-up; distribute evenly in pan.

Peel potatoes. Quarter; cut into ½-inch-thick wedges. Arrange around chicken.

Peel carrots. Cut in half lengthwise, then into sticks. Add to pan.

Peel onion; sliver. Distribute among vegetables in pan. Sprinkle garlic and lemon juice over all. Salt lightly. Grind fresh pepper over whole pan. Bake at 350°F 1 hour, basting every 15 minutes, or until chicken is cooked through and vegetables are tender.

chicken with garlic, rosemary, and white wine

Yield: 4 servings

2 tablespoons butter
2 tablespoons vegetable oil
2 or 3 cloves garlic, peeled
1 frying chicken (2½ pounds), washed, quartered, dried
1 small branch fresh rosemary, cut in half,
    or ½ teaspoon dried rosemary leaves
Salt
Fresh ground pepper
½ cup dry white wine

Use a skillet large enough to hold the chicken quarters. Heat butter and oil over medium heat. When butter foam goes down, add garlic and chicken quarters, skin-side-down. Let chicken brown on 1 side; turn pieces. Add rosemary. (Remove garlic if it is too dark.) Brown second side of chicken pieces. Add salt, pepper, and wine; let wine bubble. Reduce heat to simmer; cover. Cook about 30 minutes, until chicken is tender to a fork. (If extra liquid is needed, add water by the tablespoon.) Remove chicken to serving platter; keep warm.

Remove all but 3 tablespoons fat from skillet. On high heat add 3 tablespoons water; mix with all cooking juices. Pour over chicken. Serve at once.

chicken with sausage

Yield: 4 servings

2 pounds cut-up frying-chicken parts
3 tablespoons olive oil
4 sweet Italian sausage links (½ pound)

1 medium onion, peeled, sliced
1 large green pepper, cleaned, sliced
1 cup sliced fresh mushrooms
1 (16-ounce) can Italian-style plum tomatoes, broken up with fork

3 tablespoons tomato paste
½ cup red wine
1 teaspoon crumbled sweet basil
Pinch of sugar
Salt and pepper

Wash chicken parts; pat dry.

Heat oil in heavy skillet. Fry chicken, few pieces at a time, until golden, turning frequently. Remove from skillet; drain well.

Add sausages to skillet; prick with fork. Fry until well-browned. Remove from pan. Discard all but 3 tablespoons drippings.

Add onion, pepper, and mushrooms to skillet; saute until tender. Add tomatoes, tomato paste, wine, and seasonings; stir well. Bring to boil. Add chicken and sausage. Cover; reduce heat to low. Cook 35 to 40 minutes. Serve with plain pasta.

opposite: chicken with sausage

fettuccelle and chicken

Yield: 4 to 6 servings

2 whole chicken breasts, filleted
8 tablespoons butter
1 teaspoon olive oil
1½ teaspoons salt
Generous amount fresh-ground black pepper
1 pound fettuccelle (narrow fettuccine)

Cut chicken meat into ½-inch pieces. Place 6 tablespoons butter and olive oil in skillet. Cook diced chicken in oil mixture 15 minutes. Chicken should still be juicy. Add salt and a generous amount of fresh-ground pepper. If necessary, add more butter to keep the chicken moist. Remove; keep warm.

Cook fettuccelle *al dente*; drain. Toss with 2 tablespoons butter and half of chicken. Spoon into individual serving dishes. Top with remaining chicken sauce.

fried chicken italian

Yield: 4 servings

2½ pounds chicken parts
  (drumsticks, thighs, breasts,
  and wings)
⅓ cup flour
½ teaspoon seasoned salt
¼ teaspoon pepper

2 eggs
2 tablespoons milk
⅔ cup dry bread crumbs
⅓ cup grated Parmesan cheese
Oil for frying
Parsley
Lemon slices

Wash chicken; pat dry.

Combine flour, seasoned salt, and pepper in paper bag. Shake chicken few pieces at a time in flour mixture until lightly coated.

Beat eggs and milk together in shallow bowl.

Combine bread crumbs and cheese on waxed paper.

Dip floured chicken pieces into egg, then bread-crumb mixture; coat well.

Heat 1½ inches oil in heavy skillet over moderate heat. Fry chicken few pieces at a time until golden brown. Drain on paper towels. Place on baking sheet. Bake at 350°F 15 to 20 minutes or until juices run clear when pierced with a knife.

Garnish with parsley and lemon slices. Serve with basil-flavored tomato sauce if you wish.

linguine with chicken livers

Yield: 4 to 6 servings

2 onions, chopped
2 slices bacon, diced
2 tablespoons olive oil
1 teaspoon salt
Fresh-ground black pepper
2 cups Italian plum tomatoes
  (1-pound can)
1/8 teaspoon crushed red pepper
½ pound chicken livers, cut into
  quarters
1 tablespoon butter
1 pound linguine

In saucepan cook onions and bacon in oil until onions are soft. Add salt, pepper, and tomatoes. Use a wooden spoon to break up tomatoes. Let simmer 20 minutes. Stir in red pepper. Simmer until sauce thickens somewhat. Taste; adjust seasonings as desired.

In a medium-size skillet sauté chicken livers in melted butter about 5 minutes. Stir so livers are thoroughly cooked. Place livers and butter in the sauce. Simmer at least 5 minutes.

Cook linguine *al dente*; drain. Spoon linguine into soup bowls. Cover with sauce and livers.

opposite: linguine with chicken livers

rigatoni and chicken breast

Yield: 4 to 6 servings

1 pound rigatoni
½ chicken breast, boned
¼ pound butter
¼ pound grated Parmesan cheese
2 egg yolks, beaten
1 cup heavy cream
1 teaspoon salt
Generous amount of freshly ground pepper

Cook rigatoni in boiling salted water 10 minutes. Drain; set aside.

Grind raw chicken twice.

In heavy saucepan blend butter, half of cheese, egg yolks, cream, salt, pepper, and chicken. Stir until chicken is coated well.

Place rigatoni in large pot. Stir in hot chicken mixture; be sure sauce and pasta are well-mixed. Simmer about 15 minutes; stir occasionally. Serve in soup bowls. Sprinkle remaining cheese on top of each portion.

roast chicken with rosemary

Yield: 4 servings

3 cloves garlic, peeled
1 heaping teaspoon dried
    rosemary leaves
1 frying chicken (about 3 pounds)
    washed, dried thoroughly
Salt
Freshly ground pepper
¼ cup vegetable oil

Place garlic and ½ of rosemary into chicken cavity. Add salt and pepper to taste. Use ½ of oil to rub outside of chicken. Season with salt and more fresh-ground pepper and remaining rosemary.

Line roasting pan with remaining oil. Put chicken into pan. Bake at 375°F 1 hour on middle shelf of oven. Baste with pan juices at 15 minute intervals. When skin of chicken is well-browned and crisp, remove to heated platter.

Pour out all but 2 tablespoons of fat from roaster. Place pan on stove on high heat. Add 2 tablespoons water; scrape up residue in pan to make thin gravy. Pour over chicken; serve.

spaghettini with chicken and peas

Yield: 4 to 6 servings

1 boned chicken breast, cubed
2 tablespoons olive oil
½ teaspoon salt
Fresh-ground black pepper
1 cup (8-ounce can) baby peas
1 pound spaghettini
3 tablespoons grated Asiago
    cheese
1 egg, beaten

Place chicken in oil; sauté until golden. Season with salt and generous amount of pepper.

In saucepan heat peas in their own liquid. Drain liquid from peas into chicken. Simmer, uncovered, 5 minutes. Place peas in with chicken mixture; season with more fresh-ground pepper. Simmer 5 minutes.

Cook spaghettini al dente; drain well. Place in heated bowl.

Blend together cheese and beaten egg; pour gradually into chicken and peas. Divide in half; gently mix half with pasta. Serve in hot individual bowls; top with remaining chicken sauce.

opposite: roast chicken with rosemary

stuffed chicken

Yield: 6 servings

1 (6-pound) capon or roasting
  chicken
½ pound hot or sweet Italian
  sausage (either bulk or links
  with casings removed)
2 tablespoons olive oil
½ cup finely chopped onion

1 clove garlic, peeled, chopped
1 cup raw long-grain rice
2 cups boiling water
1 cup cleaned, sliced fresh
  mushrooms (or substitute 4-ounce
  can drained mushrooms)

1 teaspoon chicken-broth
  granules
¼ teaspoon crumbled dried sweet
  basil
Salt and pepper
Olive oil for rubbing
6 medium potatoes, peeled

Wash chicken; pat dry.

In small skillet sauté sausage in oil until lightly browned. Add onion and garlic; sauté until lightly browned. Add rice; cook, stirring, until opaque. Add water, mushrooms, broth granules, and seasonings; cover tightly. Reduce heat to low; cook 15 to 20 minutes, until tender. Cool.

Stuff chicken with mixture. Truss body cavity shut. Stuff neck cavity; skewer shut. Pin wings close to body; tie legs together. Rub liberally with oil, salt, and pepper.

Grease roasting pan; place chicken in pan. Roast at 350°F (25 minutes to the pound). One hour before chicken is done, add potatoes to roasting pan. Baste occasionally with pan juices.

turkey-breast cutlets with lemon and wine sauce

Yield: 4 servings

2 tablespoons flour
3 tablespoons freshly grated
  Parmesan cheese
½ teaspoon salt
¼ teaspoon white pepper
¼ teaspoon nutmeg
1 egg, well-beaten
½ cup milk

1 pound raw boneless turkey
  breast
Flour
4 tablespoons sweet butter
⅓ cup dry white wine
Juice of ½ lemon
Chopped fresh parsley for garnish
Lemon wedges

In shallow bowl combine flour, cheese, salt, pepper, and nutmeg. Add egg and milk; beat until well-blended.

Skin turkey breast; cut crosswise into 6 slices. Pound with meat mallet or side of plate until thin. Dredge lightly in flour; shake off excess.

Heat butter in large heavy skillet over moderate heat until foam subsides. Dip turkey in batter; fry until golden. Remove from pan; keep warm.

When all turkey is cooked, add wine to skillet. Cook over low heat 2 minutes, stirring to loosen browned bits from pan. Add lemon juice; mix well. Pour sauce over turkey cutlets; sprinkle with chopped parsley. Serve immediately with lemon wedges.

turkey tetrazzini

Yield: 6 servings

4 tablespoons butter or margarine
3 tablespoons olive oil
½ pound fresh mushrooms,
  cleaned, sliced
4 tablespoons flour

2 cups chicken broth
1 cup heavy cream
2 tablespoons dry sherry
¾ cup grated Parmesan cheese
1/8 teaspoon ground nutmeg

3 cups cubed cooked turkey
½ pound spaghetti or vermicelli,
  cooked, drained
2 tablespoons butter
¼ cup Italian-style bread crumbs

Heat 4 tablespoons butter, and oil in large saucepan. Add mushrooms; sauté 5 minutes. Remove mushrooms with slotted spoon; reserve.

Add flour to pan juices; stir to form a roux. Cook until bubbly. Slowly add chicken broth; cook until thickened. Remove from heat. Add cream, sherry, Parmesan, and nutmeg; stir until cheese melts. Add turkey and reserved mushrooms; stir well. Combine with cooked spaghetti; turn into greased 13 × 9 × 2-inch baking dish (or use 3-quart baking dish of your choice).

Melt 2 tablespoons butter; toss with bread crumbs. Sprinkle over casserole. Bake at 375°F 25 to 30 minutes.

opposite: turkey-breast cutlets with lemon and wine sauce

fish

spaghetti with clams and anchovies

Yield: 4 to 6 servings

2 white onions, peeled, chopped
2 tablespoons olive oil
30 shucked cherrystone clams and liquid
6 anchovy fillets, drained
10 ripe tomatoes, peeled, chopped
2 small green peppers, chopped
1 garlic clove, peeled, minced
1 pound spaghetti

Use medium to large saucepan to sauté onions in oil. When onions are soft and transparent, add clam liquid and anchovies. Simmer 8 minutes. Add tomatoes, green peppers, and garlic. Cook until about ½ of liquid has been absorbed, about 30 minutes. Add clams; cook 5 minutes.

Cook spaghetti *al dente*; drain. Place into warm bowl. Pour sauce over spaghetti; toss to mix. Serve in hot bowls so that every bit of sauce can be spooned up.

cod with olive and caper sauce

Yield: 4 servings

olive and caper sauce

2 tablespoons olive oil
¼ cup chopped onion
1 clove garlic, minced
1½ cups tomato puree
½ teaspoon sugar
¼ cup chopped pitted black olives
1 tablespoon drained chopped capers
½ teaspoon crumbled oregano
Pepper

1½ pounds cod fillets, defrosted if frozen

Heat oil in saucepan. Add onion and garlic; sauté until tender. Add remaining sauce ingredients; simmer 15 minutes.

Rinse fish under cold running water; pat dry. Place in lightly greased shallow baking dish in single layer. Pour sauce over fish. Bake at 350°F 25 minutes, until fish flakes easily with fork.

salt cod venetian-style

Yield: 4 or 5 servings

1½ pounds salt cod
¾ cup olive oil
2 medium onions, peeled, sliced
1 clove garlic, peeled, minced
Flour
1½ cups milk
Fresh-ground pepper
2 tablespoons chopped parsley
2 tablespoons grated Parmesan cheese

Place cod in cold water to cover. Soak 24 hours; change water several times. Drain well. Skin and bone cod. Cut into serving-size pieces.

Heat oil in heavy skillet. Add onions and garlic; sauté until tender.

Lightly dredge cod in flour. Tightly pack into shallow casserole dish. Pour onion mixture over cod. Add milk to casserole. Sprinkle with fresh-ground pepper, parsley, and cheese. Cover tightly with foil. Bake at 250°F 4½ hours; stir occasionally.

opposite: spaghetti with clams and anchovies

rolled haddock fillets

Yield: 4 servings

1¼ pounds haddock or flounder
    fillets (4 to 5 fillets)
1½ tablespoons butter
2 tablespoons chopped onion
2 tablespoons chopped celery
1 cup dry bread crumbs
1 tablespoon chopped parsley

2 tablespoons grated Parmesan cheese
½ teaspoon crumbled dried tarragon
Salt and pepper
1 egg, beaten
2 tablespoons milk
3 tablespoons butter
½ lemon, thinly sliced

Wash fish fillets; pat dry.

Heat 1½ tablespoons butter in small skillet. Sauté onion and celery in butter until tender. Remove from heat.

In bowl combine bread crumbs, parsley, cheese, tarragon, salt, and pepper; mix well. Add celery, onion, and butter; mix.

Beat egg and milk. Add to crumb mixture; thoroughly combine. Pat about ⅓ cup crumb mixture on top of each fillet; roll up like jelly roll. Fasten with toothpicks.

Melt 1½ tablespoons butter in 8-inch baking dish. Place fish rolls on end in dish. Dot with remaining butter. Top with lemon slices. Bake at 350°F 30 minutes or until fish is tender and flakes easily with a fork.

halibut with parsley sauce

Yield: 4 servings

1 quart water
½ medium yellow onion, peeled, sliced thin
1 stalk celery
2 or 3 parsley sprigs
1 bay leaf
1/8 teaspoon fennel seeds
1 cup dry white wine
½ teaspoon salt
2 pounds halibut, cut in 1 slice, bone removed

Place 1 quart water in deep saucepan. Put in onion, celery, parsley, bay leaf, fennel seeds, white wine, and salt; bring to boil. Let bubble about 15 minutes. This is the poaching liquid for the fish and it must be enough to cover the fish. If insufficient, add more water. Add fish; reduce heat to simmer. Simmer 10 to 12 minutes. When done, turn off heat but keep fish in poaching liquid until sauce is ready.

parsley sauce

1 tablespoon finely chopped
    yellow onion
2½ tablespoons butter
2 tablespoons olive oil
2 tablespoons finely chopped
    parsley
½ teaspoon finely chopped garlic
1 tablespoon chopped capers
2 teaspoons anchovy paste
2 teaspoons flour dissolved in
    ½ cup broth
2 tablespoons red wine vinegar
Salt to taste
Freshly ground pepper

garnish

2 hard-boiled eggs, sliced
1 lemon, sliced in ¼-inch rounds
Gherkins, sliced lengthwise at one end, fanned out
Parsley leaves

Lightly tan onion in 1½ tablespoons butter and the oil. Add parsley, garlic, capers, and anchovy paste. Stir and cook about 3 minutes. By tablespoons, add flour–broth mixture; stir well after each addition. Put in vinegar; stir over moderate heat to boil 2 minutes. Taste; add salt and pepper as desired. Remove from heat. Add remaining tablespoon butter.

Use two spatulas to lift fish; be careful not to break it up. Place on warm serving platter. Pour sauce over. Garnish with eggs, lemon rounds, and gherkins; sprinkle parsley leaves over all.

opposite: halibut with parsley sauce

fish and spaghetti

Yield: 4 servings

8 ounces spaghetti
1 teaspoon salt
1 quart water
1½ pounds salmon fillets
Juice of ½ lemon
2 tablespoons butter
2 small onions, diced
1 bunch soup greens, diced
1 tablespoon flour

1 cup white wine
1 cup hot beef broth
Salt to taste
Dash of sugar
White pepper to taste
8 or 9 ounces canned mussels,
    drained
1 pound tomatoes, peeled, cubed
3 ounces cheese, grated

Cook spaghetti in boiling, salted water about 20 minutes. Rinse under cold water; drain well.

Wash fish fillets; pat dry with paper toweling. Sprinkle with lemon juice.

Heat butter in pot; sauté onions and soup greens 5 minutes. Add fish. Sprinkle with flour; stir. Add wine and hot broth; simmer 5 minutes. Add salt, sugar, and pepper. Add mussels and tomatoes; cook over low heat 10 minutes.

Place spaghetti on large platter. Put fish mixture on top. Sprinkle with grated cheese.

salmon steaks italian

Yield: 6 servings

2 pounds salmon or other fish steaks, fresh or frozen
2 cups Italian dressing
2 tablespoons lemon juice
2 teaspoons salt
¼ teaspoon pepper
Paprika

Thaw steaks, if frozen; pat dry with toweling. Cut into serving-size portions; place in single layer in shallow baking dish.

Combine remaining ingredients except paprika. Pour sauce over fish. Let stand 30 minutes; turn once. Remove fish; reserve sauce for basting. Place fish in well-greased hinged wire grills or on rack in open roasting pan. Sprinkle with paprika. Cook about 4 inches from moderately hot coals or preheated broiler 8 minutes. Baste with sauce; sprinkle with paprika. Turn; cook 7 to 10 minutes, until fish flakes easily. Place on heated platter. Garnish with parsley and lemon wedges.

ziti with sardine sauce

Yield: 6 servings

sardine sauce

2 tablespoons butter
2 tablespoons olive oil
2 small white onions, peeled,
    minced
2 fresh basil leaves, minced
4 ripe tomatoes, peeled, diced
1 pound fresh sardines, cut into
    2-inch pieces

½ teaspoon salt
Generous dash of fresh-ground
    black pepper
½ cup clam juice
6 large black olives, sliced
1 tablespoon pignolia (pine nuts)

Heat butter and oil in medium-size saucepan. Add onions, basil, and tomatoes; simmer until onions are soft. Add sardine pieces. Use wooden spoon to break up tomatoes and sardines as they cook. Season with salt and pepper to taste. Add clam juice a little at a time by tablespoons; stir to blend all flavors. Simmer gently about 25 minutes. Sauce will be smooth and not watery. Add olives and pine nuts; simmer 10 minutes.

1 pound ziti tagliati

While sauce simmers, cook ziti *al dente*; drain. Place in warmed bowl. Add ½ of sauce; toss gently to blend. Spoon into individual portions. Spoon remaining sauce on top.

opposite: salmon steaks Italian

shrimp macaroni

Yield: 4 servings

2½ quarts salted water
10 ounces macaroni
10 ounces canned shrimp, drained
Juice of 1 lemon
2 tablespoons butter or margarine

1 small onion, peeled, diced
18 ounces tomato paste
2 tablespoons pickle relish
4 ounces beef broth made from cubes
Salt to taste

Freshly ground black pepper to taste
Dash of dried red pepper
½ bunch parsley, chopped fine
2 ounces Swiss cheese, grated

Bring water to boil in large pot. Add macaroni; cook 10 minutes.

Meanwhile, place shrimp in bowl; sprinkle with lemon juice.

Heat butter in skillet. Add onion; sauté until golden, about 5 minutes. Add shrimp, tomato paste, relish, and broth. Season with salt, black pepper, and red pepper. Simmer 10 minutes.

Rinse macaroni in lukewarm water; drain. Place in warmed bowl. Stir in shrimp sauce. Sprinkle with parsley. Serve cheese in separate bowl.

shrimp marinara

Yield: 3 servings

1 pound large shrimp (18 to 22)
1 quart water
Salt
1 bay leaf
1 slice lemon

Peel and devein shrimp.

Combine water, salt to taste, bay leaf, and lemon in large saucepan. Bring to boil. Add shrimp; rapidly bring water to boil. Cook 5 minutes; drain.

marinara sauce

2 tablespoons olive oil
½ cup chopped onion
1 clove garlic, minced
1½ cups Italian-style peeled plum tomatoes
¼ cup tomato puree
½ teaspoon sugar
½ teaspoon crumbled dried sweet basil
Salt and pepper

garnish

2 tablespoons dry bread crumbs
2 tablespoons grated Parmesan cheese
1 tablespoon parsley, finely chopped

Heat oil in heavy skillet. Add onion and garlic; sauté until tender. Break up tomatoes; add to onion and garlic along with tomato puree and seasonings. Reduce heat to low; cook, uncovered, 20 minutes.

Place shrimp in lightly greased au gratin dish. Top with sauce.

Combine the bread crumbs, cheese, and parsley; sprinkle over shrimp and sauce.

Preheat oven to 450°F; bake 10 minutes.

shrimp scampi

Yield: 6 servings

2 pounds large or jumbo shrimp, raw, in shells
¾ cup olive oil
2 cloves garlic, crushed
1 teaspoon salt

½ teaspoon freshly ground pepper
¼ cup chopped parsley
Lemon wedges

Wash shrimp well. Slit down back almost to tail with very sharp knife. Devein shrimp; leave shell intact. Place in single layer in shallow pan.

Combine oil, garlic, salt, and pepper; pour over shrimp. Cover; refrigerate 2 hours.

Thread 4 or 5 shrimp (depending on size) on each skewer. Grill over hot charcoal fire or in broiler (4 inches from heat source) 4 to 5 minutes on each side. Baste with oil in which shrimp were marinated.

Serve immediately, sprinkled with parsley, topped with lemon wedges.

opposite: shrimp scampi

vermicelli with shrimp

Yield: 2 servings

3½ tablespoons butter
2 cloves garlic, minced
1¼ cups shrimp, peeled,
   deveined
2 tablespoons chopped fresh
   parsley

2 tablespoons white wine
¼ cup freshly grated Parmesan
   cheese
½ cup heavy cream
Dash of freshly grated black
   pepper

4 ounces vermicelli, cooked,
   well-drained
¾ cup tiny frozen peas, cooked
   until just tender

Heat 1 tablespoon butter in large skillet. Add garlic. Cook 1 minute; stir constantly. Add shrimp, parsley, and wine. Cook until shrimp turn pink and just tender, about 2 to 3 minutes. Remove mixture to bowl.

Add remaining butter to same pan; heat until melted. Add cheese, cream, and pepper. Cook over low heat until cheese melts and sauce is smooth. Remove from heat. Add vermicelli, peas, and shrimp mixture. Gently mix until well-blended.

fish in sour sauce

Yield: 4 servings

1 pound sole fillets, defrosted
   if frozen
⅓ cup flour
Salt and white pepper
6 tablespoons olive oil

Wash fish; pat dry. Cut into serving-size pieces.

Combine flour, salt, and pepper on piece of waxed paper. Dredge fish in flour mixture.

Heat oil in heavy skillet. Over moderate heat brown fish few pieces at a time, without crowding. Drain on paper towels. Place in 9 × 9-inch glass baking dish.

sour sauce

2 tablespoons olive oil
1 medium onion, peeled, diced
1 carrot, peeled, diced
1 stalk celery, diced
½ cup white wine

½ cup white wine vinegar
1 bay leaf
1 teaspoon sugar
Salt
White pepper

Heat oil in another skillet. Add onion, carrot, and celery. Cook, stirring constantly, until tender but not browned. Add wine, vinegar, and seasonings; mix well.

1½ tablespoons pine nuts
1½ tablespoons dark raisins,
   soaked in warm water to plump

Pour sauce over fish. Sprinkle with pine nuts and raisins. Cover tightly; refrigerate at least 4 hours before serving. Remove bay leaf; serve at room temperature with crisp bread as luncheon dish or antipasto.

fried squid

Yield: 4 or 5 servings

3 pounds frozen squid
2 cups Italian-style bread crumbs
1 teaspoon salt
½ teaspoon pepper
3 eggs, well-beaten

Thaw squid. Remove tentacles by cutting them from head; reserve. Remove and discard head, chitinous pen, and viscera. Wash thoroughly; drain. Cut mantle into rings.

Combine bread crumbs, salt, and pepper. Dip tentacles and mantle rings in egg, then in crumbs; coat well. Deep-fat fry at 350°F until golden brown. Serve immediately with lemon wedges.

opposite: fish in sour sauce

rice with squid

Yield: 4 servings

2 pounds squid
¼ cup olive oil
1 medium onion, peeled, chopped
2 cloves garlic, peeled, minced
½ cup white wine
Salt and pepper

1 cup raw long-grain rice
1½ cups fish stock or chicken broth
Several strands saffron
1 teaspoon hot water
2 teaspoons chopped parsley
2 tablespoons butter

Thaw squid if frozen. Remove tentacles by cutting from head; reserve. Remove and discard head, chitinous pen, and viscera. Wash thoroughly; drain. Cut mantle into thin rings.

Heat oil in large skillet. Add onion and garlic; sauté until tender. Add squid rings, tentacles, and wine. Season with salt and pepper. Cover; simmer 20 minutes. Add rice and stock; mix well. Bring mixture to boil over moderate heat. Cover; reduce heat to low. Cook 20 minutes.

Dissolve saffron in hot water; stir into fish and rice. Add parsley and butter, cut into small chunks. Season with salt and pepper to taste; serve.

tuna risotto

Yield: 4 or 5 servings

risotto

4 tablespoons oil
½ Bermuda onion, finely chopped
1½ cups long-grain rice
2 pints chicken stock, or bouillon cubes and water

Heat oil in pan. Add onion; sauté until transparent. Add rice; stir over low heat until just golden. Remove from heat. Add hot stock; stir. Return to heat; cover. Cook until rice is tender.

tuna sauce

2 tablespoons oil
2 tablespoons butter or margarine
½ Bermuda onion, finely chopped
2 tablespoons tomato puree
3 tablespoons wine vinegar
2 tablespoons lemon juice
1 (7- to 8-ounce) can tuna, flaked

Heat oil and butter in pan. Add onion; cook until soft and golden. Add tomato puree, vinegar, lemon juice, tuna, and a little oil from fish; mix well. Heat through. Adjust seasoning to taste.

Grated cheese

Stir sauce into risotto just before serving. Add a little grated cheese; serve extra cheese separately.

tuna sauce for spaghetti

Yield: 4 servings

6 tablespoons butter
6 tablespoons olive oil
2 (7-ounce) cans tuna packed in olive oil
⅓ cup chopped parsley

2 tablespoons chopped capers
2 tablespoons lemon juice
¼ cup chicken broth
Salt and pepper

Heat butter and oil over moderate heat in heavy skillet.

Meanwhile, drain tuna; finely chop.

When butter has melted, add tuna, parsley, and capers. Heat through; stir occasionally. Stir in lemon juice, broth, salt, and pepper.

Cook 1 pound spaghetti or your favorite pasta al dente. Drain well. Place in large heated bowl. Add sauce; toss gently. Serve immediately.

opposite: rice with squid

mixed fish fry

Yield: 6 servings (fish only); 4 servings (fish and vegetables)

batter

3 large eggs
¼ cup olive oil
¼ cup all-purpose flour
¼ teaspoon crumbled dried rosemary
¼ teaspoon crumbled dried sweet basil
Salt and pepper

Beat eggs with wire whip until well-mixed. Add oil; beat to mix well. Add flour and seasonings; beat until smooth batter is formed. Let stand 30 minutes. Beat again before dipping fish.

fish fry

1½ pounds fish fillets, shrimp, cleaned squid, clams,
mussels, or eel (if fish is frozen, defrost and drain
well)
Oil for frying (half olive oil if possible)
½ cup flour
Salt and pepper
Parsley, lemon wedges, and quartered tomatoes

Rinse fish; pat dry.
Heat 3 inches oil in deep-fat fryer or 1 inch oil in electric skillet to 360°F.
Dredge fish in flour seasoned with salt and pepper. Coat well; shake off excess. Dip fish in batter few pieces at a time. Deep-fat fry until golden. Drain on absorbent paper. Keep warm until all fish is cooked. Garnish with parsley and lemon wedges.
Vegetables also are delicious cooked in this manner. Trim and slice 1 medium zucchini and ¼ pound mushrooms. Cut amount of fish to be cooked to ¾ pound. Cook as above. Serve with your favorite sauce.

seafood linguine

Yield: 4 to 6 servings

¼ pound butter or margarine
2 cans minced clams, drained
1 clove garlic, minced fine
1 teaspoon salt

¼ teaspoon pepper
½ pound shrimp, cooked, deveined
2 teaspoons lemon juice
1 pound linguine, cooked

Melt butter in medium skillet. Add all ingredients (except linguine) in order given. Cook on low heat 15 minutes; stir occasionally. Pour over cooked linguine.

shrimp, lobster, and crab diavolo

Yield: 4 or 5 servings

1 (1¼-pound) live lobster
1 pound king crab legs
2 pounds medium shrimp, raw
½ cup butter
2 tablespoons olive oil

2 cloves garlic, peeled, minced
1/8 teaspoon crushed red pepper
Juice of 1 lemon
2 tablespoons chopped parsley

Steam lobster and crab legs; cool.
Peel shrimp; leave tails intact. Butterfly; remove sand vein. Drain well.
Remove lobster and crab from shells; slice. Heat butter and oil in large heavy skillet over moderate heat. Add garlic; sauté 2 minutes. Add shrimp and pepper; sauté until shrimp turns pink. Add crab and lobster; heat through. Sprinkle with lemon juice and parsley. Serve with garlic bread.

Note: You can substitute any combination of shellfish you prefer in this dish. Count on a 50 percent loss for shells (meaning: use 2 pounds raw shellfish, shells removed).

opposite: mixed fish fry

fish soup

Although this dish is called a soup, it is really more of a stew. Serve with lots of crisp-crusted Italian bread or bread sticks.

Yield: 6 to 8 servings

3 quarts water
1 tablespoon salt
1 large onion, sliced
1 bay leaf
3 stalks celery (with tops), chopped
1 (1¼-pound) lobster
½ pound shrimp
3 pounds fish heads, bones, and
  trimmings
1 dozen clams
½ cup olive oil
2 cloves garlic, peeled, minced
2 pounds fish fillets (any firm whitefish can be used;
  select one or more kinds from this list of possibilities:
  red snapper, bass, rockfish, cod, haddock, flounder,
  or perch), cut into chunks

2 cups drained Italian-style
  tomatoes, broken up
1 cup dry white wine
½ cup chopped parsley
¼ teaspoon thyme
1 teaspoon crumbled dried sweet basil
Freshly ground pepper
Scant ¼ teaspoon saffron

In large stock pot (5 to 6 quarts) combine water, salt, onion, bay leaf, and celery; bring to boil. Add lobster; return to boil. Reduce heat to low; cook 10 minutes. Add shrimp; cook 5 minutes. Remove shrimp and lobster. Add fish heads and trimmings; cook, uncovered, 1 hour.

When shrimp and lobster are cool enough to handle, remove shrimp from shells; add shells to stock. Remove sand veins; discard.

Clean lobster; remove shell. Add shell to stock. Cut meat into large chunks.

Scrub clams; wash well to remove grit. Add to stock; cook 15 minutes. Remove from pot; reserve.

Heat oil in Dutch oven. Add garlic; saute until lightly browned. Add fish; brown in oil. Add tomatoes, wine, parsley, thyme, basil, and pepper; stir well.

Strain fish stock through fine sieve. You should have 2 quarts.

Dissolve saffron in broth. Add to fish and tomato mixture; bring to boil. Reduce heat to low; cook 15 minutes. Add lobster, shrimp, and clams; cook 10 minutes. Serve in large soup bowls.

fish stew

Yield: 4 servings

5 tablespoons olive oil
1 clove garlic, minced
1 pound (4 medium) potatoes,
  peeled, diced
1 pound firm-fleshed whitefish
  (flounder, cod, or snapper),
  cut into chunks
4 cups fish stock
1 (16-ounce) can Italian-style
  tomatoes, pureed or sieved
½ cup white wine
½ teaspoon crushed fennel seed
1 bay leaf
1 teaspoon salt
1/8 teaspoon crushed red pepper
Freshly ground black pepper
3 tablespoons chopped parsley

Heat oil in Dutch oven. Add garlic; saute until well-browned; discard. Add potatoes; cook, stirring constantly, until lightly browned. Add fish, stock, tomatoes, wine, and seasonings; bring to boil. Reduce heat to low; simmer 20 to 25 minutes, until fish and potatoes are tender. Ladle into soup bowls. Sprinkle with parsley. Serve with garlic toast.

meats

beef braised with cloves

Yield: 8 servings

1 (4-pound) beef rump or
  bottom-round roast
12 cloves
Salt and freshly ground pepper
3 tablespoons olive oil
½ cup chopped onion
¼ cup chopped celery
¼ cup chopped carrot

1 clove garlic, peeled, chopped
½ cup dry red wine
2 cups beef broth
½ cup tomato sauce
1 teaspoon crumbled oregano
1 bay leaf
4 slices bacon

Wipe roast with damp cloth. Stud with cloves; rub with salt and pepper.

Heat oil in Dutch oven. Brown meat well on all sides. Remove from pan; drain off excess fat.

To Dutch oven add onion, celery, carrot, and garlic; saute until tender. Add wine, broth, tomato sauce, oregano, and bay leaf; bring to boil. Reduce heat to low. Place roast in pan. Place bacon on roast. Cover; simmer 3 hours.

Slice meat; serve with pan juices, accompanied by plain pasta or potatoes.

beef parma-style

Yield: 4 or 5 servings

1½ pounds beef round steak
½ cup dry bread crumbs
⅓ cup grated Parmesan cheese
1 egg
2 tablespoons water
¼ cup flour

⅓ cup cooking oil
1 medium onion, minced
1 (6-ounce) can tomato paste
2 cups hot water
½ teaspoon crumbled dried
  marjoram

1 teaspoon salt
¼ teaspoon pepper
½ pound mozzarella cheese, thinly
  sliced

Place meat between sheets of waxed paper; pound with heavy skillet on hard surface until quite thin. Cut into serving-size pieces.

Combine bread crumbs and Parmesan cheese.

Beat egg and 2 tablespoons water together.

Dip meat in flour; turn to coat; shake off excess. Dip meat in egg mixture, then in crumb mixture. Pat crumbs into meat to coat well.

Heat oil in heavy skillet over moderate heat. Brown the meat on both sides. Remove from pan.

Add onion to pan; brown lightly. Add tomato paste, hot water, and seasonings; stir well. Boil 5 minutes.

Place meat in shallow baking dish. Cover with sauce; reserve ¾ cup. Top meat with mozzarella cheese. Pour remaining sauce over cheese. Cover with aluminum foil. Bake at 350°F 2 hours. Serve with pasta and a green salad.

beef rolls with tomato gravy

Yield: 4 servings

1¼ pounds very thinly sliced top
  round of beef (¼ inch thick)
¼ cup olive oil
1 medium onion, finely chopped
¾ cup Italian-style bread crumbs
3 tablespoons olive oil

2 tablespoons chopped onion
1½ cups canned Italian-style peeled
  plum tomatoes, broken up
½ cup tomato sauce
½ tablespoon dehydrated parsley
  flakes

½ teaspoon sugar
½ teaspoon oregano
Salt and pepper

Pound meat well; cut into rectangular pieces approximately 4 × 6 inches. You should have 8 pieces, so vary the measurements accordingly. Heat ¼ cup olive oil in small skillet. Saute onion until tender. Remove from heat. Add bread crumbs; stir well. Place 2 tablespoons bread-crumb mixture on each piece of meat; roll jelly-roll fashion to enclose stuffing. Fasten with toothpicks.

Heat 3 tablespoons olive oil in heavy skillet. Brown steak rolls. Place in shallow baking dish.

Add onion to skillet; brown lightly. Add remaining ingredients; stir well. Simmer 15 to 20 minutes or until thickened. Pour over the steak rolls; cover. Bake at 350°F 1 hour. Serve with mashed potatoes.

opposite: beef rolls with tomato gravy

beef stew

Yield: 4 servings

2 tablespoons olive oil
2 slices bacon, chopped
½ cup chopped onion
½ cup sliced celery
1 clove garlic, minced
1¼ pounds lean stew beef, cut into
  1-inch cubes

2 tablespoons chopped parsley
1 (16-ounce) can peeled tomatoes,
  broken up
½ cup water
1 teaspoon beef-broth granules
½ teaspoon crumbled dried sweet
  basil

Salt and pepper
½ teaspoon sugar
3 medium carrots, peeled, sliced
3 medium potatoes, peeled, diced
¼ cup red wine
1½ cups sliced zucchini squash
  (unpeeled)

Heat oil in Dutch oven. Add bacon; sauté until crisp. With slotted spoon remove bacon from pan; reserve. Add onion, celery, and garlic to pan; sauté 5 minutes. Remove with slotted spoon; reserve.

Add stew beef to pan. Cook over moderate heat until well-browned on all sides; stir occasionally. Add reserved ingredients, parsley, tomatoes, water, beef-broth granules, and seasonings. Cook, covered, over low heat 1 hour. Add carrots and potatoes; stir well. Cover; cook 45 minutes. Add wine and zucchini; stir well. Cook 15 minutes or until vegetables are tender.

steak with tomato sauce

This recipe is excellent for disguising a less-tender steak.

Yield: 4 servings

tomato sauce

2 tablespoons olive oil
1 small onion, peeled, minced
2 cloves garlic, peeled, minced
1 (16-ounce) can Italian-style tomatoes
1 teaspoon crumbled oregano
Salt and pepper

Heat oil in small skillet. Add onion and garlic; sauté until tender. Break up tomatoes with fork to form small chunks. Add tomatoes, oregano, salt, and pepper to skillet; stir well. Cover; simmer 15 minutes, until sauce begins to thicken.

2 tablespoons olive oil
3 pounds T-bone, porterhouse, or sirloin steak,
  1 inch thick

Heat oil in large heavy skillet until very hot. Add steak; brown quickly on both sides; turn several times. Pour tomato sauce over steak; cover. Cook over low heat approximately 10 minutes (until done to taste). Remove steak from skillet; carve. Serve topped with tomato sauce.

stuffed peppers

Yield: 4 servings

4 medium bell peppers
1 pound ground beef
½ cup chopped onion
½ teaspoon garlic powder
1 teaspoon crumbled mixed Italian
  herbs
Salt and pepper

1 (16-ounce) can stewed tomatoes
1 (8-ounce) can tomato sauce
¼ cup water
1 cup instant rice (or quick-cooking)
2 ounces thinly sliced mozzarella
  cheese

Cut tops off peppers; remove seeds and membranes. Parboil peppers 5 minutes; drain.

Sauté beef and onion in large skillet until lightly browned; add a little oil if meat is very lean. Add garlic powder, Italian herbs, salt, pepper, tomatoes, ½ can of tomato sauce, water, and rice; stir well. Bring to boil. Reduce heat to low; cook, covered, 15 minutes.

Place peppers in 2-quart casserole. Stuff with meat mixture; spoon remaining mixture around peppers. Top with remaining tomato sauce. Cover; cook 30 minutes at 350°F. Uncover; top with cheese. Cook 10 minutes.

opposite: stuffed peppers

lamb chops venetian-style

Yield: 4 servings

2 tablespoons butter or margarine
2 tablespoons olive oil
4 lamb shoulder chops (approximately 2 pounds)
Salt and pepper to taste

1 medium onion
1¾-pound eggplant
3 tablespoons tomato paste
½ teaspoon crumbled dried sweet
   basil

½ cup boiling water
½ 10-ounce package frozen peas
1 (8½-ounce) can artichoke bottoms
   (or substitute 1 can artichoke
   hearts), drained

Heat butter and oil in heavy skillet.

Wipe chops with damp cloth; season with salt and pepper. Sauté in butter and oil approximately 4 minutes per side, until well-browned and almost done. Remove from pan; keep warm.

While chops cook, peel onion; quarter; separate layers.

Cut stem from eggplant; cut in half lengthwise; thinly slice.

Add the onion to skillet; sauté 5 minutes. Add eggplant.

Combine tomato paste, basil, and boiling water; stir well. Add to skillet; bring to boil. Reduce heat to low; cover. Cook 15 minutes. Add peas, artichoke bottoms (quartered) or hearts, and lamb chops. Cook, covered, 15 minutes or until vegetables are done through.

lamb roast roman-style

Yield: 4 or 5 servings

1 (3-pound) boned, rolled lamb roast (leg or shoulder)
2 cloves garlic, peeled, cut into slivers
1 teaspoon crumbled dry rosemary
½ teaspoon crumbled dry marjaram
Freshly ground pepper
3 slices bacon, cut in half

anchovy sauce
2 anchovy fillets
1½ tablespoons olive oil
1½ tablespoons lemon juice
1 tablespoon fresh bread crumbs
½ cup chopped parsley
1 teaspoon freshly grated lemon rind
½ teaspoon crumbled rosemary

Wipe meat with damp cloth. Cut slits in top; place garlic sliver in each slit. Rub roast with rosemary, marjoram, and pepper. Place in roast pan, fat-side-up. Place bacon slices, slightly overlapping, over top of roast. Roast at 325°F 2¼ hours (internal temperature of 170°F). Roast should still be pink when sliced.

Prepare sauce while lamb cooks. Mash anchovy fillets with oil. Stir in lemon juice and bread crumbs. Add remaining ingredients; stir well. Refrigerate until ready for use.

Serve lamb with sauce, steamed broccoli, and tomato salad. Pototoes can be pan-roasted with lamb.

roast leg of lamb with rosemary

Yield: 6 servings

1 (5-pound) whole leg of lamb or sirloin half leg of lamb
1 large clove garlic
1 teaspoon crumbled dried rosemary
1 teaspoon grated lemon peel
Salt and freshly ground black pepper
Olive oil

Wipe meat with damp cloth.

Peel garlic; rub over surface of lamb. Cut garlic clove into slivers.

Make 4 or 5 deep slashes in meat; insert garlic slivers. Rub meat with rosemary, lemon peel, salt, and pepper. Place in open roasting pan on trivet, fat-side-up. Sprinkle with olive oil. Roast at 325°F 3 hours or to an internal temperature of 180° F. Let stand 10 minutes before carving.

Peeled potatoes and carrots can be placed in pan drippings for last 1½ hours of cooking time; turn occasionally.

opposite: lamb chops—venetian-style

breaded pork chops

Yield: 4 servings

4 loin pork chops, 1 inch thick
Salt and pepper
1 large egg
2 tablespoons water
Bread crumbs
¼ cup clarified butter
½ teaspoon dried sage

Carefully trim excess fat from pork chops. Season with salt and pepper.
Beat egg and water together.
Dip chops in egg, then coat with bread crumbs; press crumbs firmly onto chops.
In heavy skillet heat butter over moderate heat.
Crumble sage; add to butter. Add chops; cook slowly until well-browned and done through.

Note: 1 pound of well-pounded veal cutlets can be substituted for pork chops.

pork chops cacciatore

Polenta, gnocchi, rice, or mashed potatoes goes well with this dish. It's delicious with the gravy!

Yield: 4 servings

2 tablespoons olive oil
4 loin pork chops (1 pound)
1 small onion, sliced
1 clove garlic, minced
½ cup sliced green pepper
1 (4-ounce) can sliced mushrooms, drained
1 (16-ounce) can peeled tomatoes, broken up with a fork
2 tablespoons sherry
½ teaspoon crumbled dried oregano
½ teaspoon crumbled dried basil
½ teaspoon sugar
Salt and pepper

Heat oil in large skillet. Brown chops well; remove from skillet.
Add onion, garlic, and green pepper to skillet; sauté lightly over medium heat. Add mushrooms, tomatoes, sherry, and seasonings; bring to boil. Return chops to skillet; cover. Simmer 1 hour or until chops are tender. Serve with pan juices.

pork roast in chianti

Yield: 6 to 8 servings

1 (4-pound) boned, rolled, tied pork roast
1½ cups Chianti wine
1 clove garlic, minced
2 tablespoons lemon juice
1 teaspoon crumbled dried rosemary
1 teaspoon crumbled dried basil
3 tablespoons olive oil
1 (8-ounce) can tomato sauce
Salt and pepper to taste

Wipe pork roast with damp cloth. Place in glass or porcelain container or heavy-duty freezer bag.
Combine Chianti, garlic, lemon juice, rosemary, and basil; pour over meat. Cover; marinate in refrigerator 24 hours. Turn occasionally (if using plastic bag, close with twist-tie). Bring roast to room temperature before cooking. Remove roast from marinade; pat dry. Reserve marinade.
Heat oil in large heavy Dutch oven. Brown roast well on all sides.
Combine marinade and tomato sauce, salt, and pepper; pour over meat. Bring to boil. Reduce heat to simmer; cover. Cook 3 hours (meat should be fork-tender). Place roast on platter; slice. Serve with pan juices.

opposite: breaded pork chops

italian sausages and beans

Yield: 4 servings

1 pound sweet or hot Italian sausage links
Cold water
2 tablespoons olive oil
¼ cup chopped onion
1 (8-ounce) can tomato sauce
2 (16-ounce) cans cannelli or kidney beans, drained
2 tablespoons chopped parsley

Prick sausages well on all sides. Place in large skillet; just barely cover with cold water. Cook over moderate heat, uncovered, until water evaporates. Then cook, turning occasionally, until sausages are browned on all sides. Remove from pan; keep warm.

Add oil and onion to skillet; sauté until tender. Add tomato sauce; simmer 5 minutes. Add beans and sausages; simmer 15 minutes; stir occasionally to prevent sticking. Sprinkle with parsley; serve.

sausage and vegetable bake

Yield: 4 servings

1 pound sweet Italian sausage links
4 medium baking potatoes, peeled, quartered, cut into
   ½-inch wedges
1 large green pepper, cleaned, cut into thin strips
1 medium onion, peeled, slivered
Salt and pepper

Pour ½ inch water into 13 × 9 × 2-inch baking dish.

Prick sausage links in several places; cut apart. Evenly distribute sausage links in baking pan. Surround them with potatoes, pepper, and onion. Salt and pepper lightly. Bake at 350°F 1 hour, basting occasionally, or until sausages are browned and potatoes are cooked through.

sausage with lentils

This dish is traditionally served in Italy on New Year's Day and is said to bring good luck!

Yield: 6 servings

2 cups dried lentils
8 cups water
1 ounce salt pork, diced
2 large tomatoes, peeled, diced
1 garlic clove, peeled
1 bay leaf
2 teaspoons salt
Freshly ground pepper
1 cotechino sausage or 1 zampone
   (about 2 pounds)

Wash lentils; pick over well to remove foreign matter. Place lentils in large saucepan. Add water, salt pork, tomatoes, garlic, bay leaf, salt, and pepper. Bring to boil over moderate heat. Skim foam from surface of cooking liquid; reduce heat to low. Simmer, uncovered; stir occasionally until lentils are soft and liquid almost evaporated. (Cooking time should be 45 minutes to 1 hour.) If liquid evaporates too quickly, add a little water.

Meanwhile, prick sausage well. Place in large pot; add water to cover. Bring to boil. Reduce heat to low; simmer 1 hour, until tender. Remove from pan; cool slightly. Slice; place on platter.

Remove bay leaf and garlic clove from lentils. Spoon lentils around sausage; serve.

Note: Cotechino and zampone are usually available in Italian delicatessens around the New Year. If unavailable, substitute 1½ pounds Italian sausage. Prick well; cook in ½ inch water until water evaporates; brown in own fat.

opposite: sausage with lentils

milanese veal rolls

Yield: 4 servings

1½ pounds rump roast of veal or veal cutlet
Salt and pepper
Ground sage
4 slices prosciutto
8 thin slices mozzarella cheese

3 tablespoons olive oil
1 small onion, chopped
1 clove garlic, minced
1 (16-ounce) can Italian-style peeled tomatoes
½ cup white wine

Salt and pepper
8 thin strips mozzarella cheese
Parsley sprigs

Pound meat with mallet to 1/8 inch thickness. Sprinkle with salt, pepper, and a little sage. Cut into 8 rectangular pieces.

Cut prosciutto slices in half.

Top veal pieces with piece of ham and slice of mozzarella. Roll jelly-roll fashion; tie with string.

Heat oil in large skillet; sauté veal rolls until browned. Remove from pan.

Add onion and garlic to pan; sauté until tender.

Break up tomatoes with fork. Add to skillet, with wine, salt, and pepper; mix well. Add veal rolls; cover. Simmer 1½ hours or until tender. Top with mozzarella strips; cover. Melt cheese.

Serve on a bed of hot cooked spaghetti, topped with sauce and garnished with parsley sprigs.

stuffed breast of veal

Yield: 6 servings

stuffing

3 tablespoons olive oil
1 medium onion, chopped
½ pound fresh spinach, stems removed, shredded
¼ pound ground veal
¼ pound ground pork
1 egg
½ cup fresh bread crumbs
¼ cup fresh pine nuts
1/8 teaspoon nutmeg
Salt and pepper

veal

1 (4- to 5-pound) veal breast, boned
Salt and pepper
2 tablespoons olive oil
2 cups beef broth
½ cup white wine
1 carrot, peeled, sliced
1 stalk celery, chopped
2 bay leaves
Salt and pepper
3 tablespoons cornstarch
3 tablespoons water

Heat oil in heavy skillet. Add onion; sauté until tender. Add spinach; sauté, stirring constantly, until wilted. Remove from heat; cool. Add remaining stuffing ingredients; mix well.

Have butcher cut pocket in veal breast for stuffing. Wipe meat with damp cloth. Season with salt and pepper on outside and in pocket. Fill pocket with stuffing; skewer shut. Heat oil in Dutch oven. Brown veal well on all sides. Add broth, wine, carrot, celery, and seasonings. Bring to boil; cover. Roast at 350°F 2½ hours; baste every ½ hour. Remove from oven. Take meat from pan; keep warm.

Combine cornstarch and water; mix well. Add to pan juices; cook over low heat until thickened.

Remove skewer; carve veal breast. Serve with gravy.

veal chops milanese

Yield: 4 servings

4 veal sirloin chops, about 6 ounces each (1½ pounds total)
⅓ cup flour
Salt and pepper
2 eggs, beaten

⅔ cup dry bread crumbs
⅓ cup grated Parmesan cheese
¼ cup olive oil
2 tablespoons butter

Wipe veal with damp cloth.

Combine flour, salt, and pepper on piece of waxed paper. Dredge chops in flour mixture; shake off excess. Dip in eggs, then in mixture of bread crumbs and cheese; coat well.

Combine oil and butter in large heavy skillet; heat until foam subsides. Add chops; cook over moderate heat, turning occasionally, until golden brown. Drain on paper towels. Serve immediately.

Garnish with lemon slices. Serve with browned butter or tomato sauce if desired.

opposite: milanese veal rolls

veal scallopini in lemon sauce

Yield: 4 servings

1¼ pounds veal for scallopini
2½ tablespoons flour
Salt
White pepper
6 tablespoons clarified butter

¼ cup chicken broth
¼ cup white wine
½ fresh lemon, thinly sliced
1 tablespoon finely chopped parsley

Arrange veal slices close together on cutting board or waxed paper. Lightly sprinkle with flour, salt, and white pepper. Turn; flour and season other side of meat.

Heat clarified butter in large heavy skillet. Quickly brown veal a few pieces at a time on both sides. Remove from pan; keep meat warm.

Add chicken broth, wine, and lemon slices to skillet. Push lemon slices down into liquid. Reduce heat to simmer; cover pan. Cook over low heat 5 minutes.

Place veal on heated platter. Pour sauce over meat. Sprinkle with parsley.

veal shanks milanese

Yield: 4 servings

gremolata

3 pounds veal shank, sawed into
   thick slices with marrow intact
Salt and pepper
Flour
6 tablespoons butter
1 medium onion, peeled, chopped
1 clove garlic, peeled, minced

2 carrots, peeled, diced
2 stalks celery, chopped
½ cup white wine
¼ cup chicken broth
1 bay leaf
¼ teaspoon thyme

2 tablespoons finely chopped
   parsley
1 clove garlic, peeled, finely minced
1 teaspoon finely grated lemon peel

Wipe veal with damp cloth. Season with salt and pepper. Dredge in flour; shake off excess.

Heat butter in deep skillet or Dutch oven. Add veal; brown well on all sides. Remove from pan.

Add onion and garlic to pan; sauté until tender. Add vegetables, wine, chicken broth, and seasonings. Add veal shanks, standing on their sides to prevent marrow falling from bone during cooking. Bring mixture to boil. Cover pan tightly; reduce heat to simmer. Cook approximately 1 hour, until veal is tender. If mixture looks dry at any time, add a little broth.

Meanwhile, combine gremolata ingredients; mix well.

Transfer veal to heated platter. Pour sauce over meat; sprinkle with gremolata. Serve with risotto or plain cooked pasta.

veal with marsala wine

Yield: 4 servings

1 pound thinly sliced leg of veal *or* 1 pound tenderized
   unbreaded veal steaks
2 eggs
½ cup flour
Salt and pepper
5 tablespoons butter (divided)
1 cup thinly sliced fresh mushrooms
⅓ cup marsala wine
⅔ cup beef broth

Lightly pound veal to an even thickness.

Beat eggs well in shallow pie plate. Place meat in egg mixture. Let stand 30 minutes; turn occasionally.

Combine flour, salt, and pepper to taste.

Drain veal; dredge in flour mixture.

Heat 3 tablespoons butter in heavy skillet over medium heat until hot and foamy. Add veal; sauté, turning, until golden brown. Remove veal from pan; keep warm on platter.

Melt remaining butter in skillet. Sauté mushrooms until tender. Add wine and beef broth; cook 5 minutes. Pour over veal.

opposite: veal shanks milanese

mixed boiled meats with green sauce

Yield: 4 generous servings

meat pot

1 pound beef pot roast or brisket
1 pound veal shoulder
2 whole chicken legs
2 marrow bones, cracked
Water
2 bay leaves
1 onion
2 cloves

1 clove garlic
1 teaspoon salt
½ teaspoon sugar
4 peppercorns
½ teaspoon thyme
4 carrots, peeled, cut in half
　　lengthwise

2 leeks, cleaned, cut in half
　　lengthwise
½ pound cooked beef tongue
Parsley for garnish

Place beef, veal, chicken, and marrow bones in large Dutch oven or stew pot. Cover with water. Add bay leaves. Peel onion; stud with cloves. Add to kettle.

Peel the garlic clove. Sprinkle with salt; mash with knife blade. Add to pot, with sugar, peppercorns, and thyme; bring to boil. Skim foam from surface of liquid. Reduce heat to low; cover. Cook 40 minutes. Remove chicken. Add carrots and leeks; cook 30 minutes.

green sauce

Juice of 1 fresh lemon
3 egg yolks
¼ teaspoon salt
½ cup olive oil
1 slice white bread, soaked in water,
　　squeezed dry
½ teaspoon prepared mustard
1 clove garlic, peeled, mashed
½ cup chopped parsley
½ teaspoon crumbled dried sweet
　　basil
½ teaspoon crumbled dried oregano

Meanwhile, make green sauce. Combine lemon juice, egg yolks, and salt in jar of electric blender. Blend on medium speed 2 minutes. Add oil a tablespoon at a time; blend well after each addition. Add bread, mustard, and garlic; blend 2 minutes. Pour into serving bowl. Stir in parsley, basil, and oregano. Refrigerate until serving time.

Skin chicken. Return to pot, along with tongue; heat through. Remove meats from pot; slice. Arrange on warm platter. Garnish with parsley. Serve with green sauce. Reserve broth for soups.

meat sauce for spaghetti

Yield: 4 servings

¼ cup olive oil
1 medium onion, finely chopped
2 cloves garlic, peeled, minced
¾ pound lean ground beef
½ pound bulk Italian sausage
　　(sweet or hot)
1 (28-ounce) can Italian-style plum
　　tomatoes (sieved or blenderized)
1 (6-ounce) can tomato paste
1 (6-ounce) can water
½ cup dry red wine
1 teaspoon crumbled mixed Italian
　　herbs
1 teaspoon sugar
1/8 teaspoon crushed red pepper
Salt and pepper

Heat oil in large heavy saucepan. Add onion and garlic; sauté until tender. Add beef and sausage; cook, breaking into small chunks, until lightly browned. Drain well. Add remaining ingredients; mix well. Bring to boil; reduce heat to simmer. Cook, partially covered, 2 hours, until thick. Serve over hot cooked spaghetti or macaroni.

opposite: meat sauce for spaghetti

vegetables

stuffed artichokes roman-style

Yield: 4 servings

4 large artichokes
1 lemon
¾ cup dry bread crumbs
¾ cup fresh-grated Romano or Parmesan cheese
2 cloves garlic, peeled, finely minced
3 tablespoons minced parsley
1 tablespoon crumbled dried mint
Salt and pepper
1½ sticks (12 tablespoons) butter, melted

Wash artichokes. Break off stems; discard. Discard discolored outer leaves. With sharp knife cut off top of artichoke 1 inch below tip. Snip off sharp tips of leaves. Trim artichoke base with knife so it sits flat and level. Rub cut surfaces with lemon.

In stainless steel or enamel pot bring 2½ inches water to rolling boil. Add juice of ½ lemon. Add artichokes. Cover; cook 15 minutes. Drain upside down in bowl. Pull out centers of artichokes; with small spoon scrape out the choke.

Combine bread crumbs, cheese, garlic, parsley, mint, salt, and pepper; mix well. Stuff mixture between leaves and into center of each artichoke. Place artichokes upright in large saucepan, tightly packed in pan. Drizzle each with 3 tablespoons melted butter; be sure to get butter between leaves. Add ½ inch hot water to pan. Bring to boil over moderate heat; cover. Bake at 400°F 1 hour, until artichokes are tender.

asparagus milanese-style

Yield: 3 servings

1 (10-ounce) package frozen asparagus spears,
  partially thawed
1 tablespoon melted butter or margarine (divided)
2 tablespoons dry sherry
½ teaspoon seasoned salt-and-pepper mixture
⅓ cup Italian-style bread crumbs
2 tablespoons grated Romano cheese

Preheat oven to 350°F.

Separate asparagus spears; place in 9-inch pie plate.

Mix butter, sherry, and salt and pepper mixture; pour over asparagus. Tightly cover with foil. Bake 30 minutes or until crisp-tender. Uncover; drain liquid from asparagus.

Melt remaining butter; combine with crumbs. Sprinkle over asparagus. Sprinkle with cheese. Broil until crumbs are lightly browned and cheese is melted.

romano beans in tomato sauce

Yield: 3 or 4 servings

2 tablespoons olive oil
1 small garlic clove, minced
2 tablespoons chopped onion
¼ cup minced prosciutto or baked ham
½ cup tomato sauce
Salt and pepper
2 tablespoons water
1 (9-ounce) package frozen Italian
  (or Romano) green beans

Heat oil in medium saucepan. Add garlic, onion, and prosciutto; sauté 5 minutes. Add tomato sauce, salt, pepper, and water; mix well. Add frozen beans; bring to boil. Stir to break up beans; cover. Reduce heat to low; cook 15 minutes.

opposite: romano beans in tomato sauce

eggplant parmigiana

A whole meal in itself!

Yield: 8 servings

tomato sauce

¼ cup olive oil
1 pound ground round steak (or
   lean ground beef)
1 medium onion, chopped
1 clove garlic, peeled, chopped

½ cup chopped celery
½ cup chopped green pepper
1 (15-ounce) can tomato sauce
1 (6-ounce) can tomato paste

1 (16-ounce) can Italian plum
   tomatoes, broken up with fork
¾ teaspoon crumbled mixed Italian
   seasoning

eggplant and filling

1 medium eggplant
1 egg
2 tablespoons water
Fine dry bread crumbs

½ cup cooking oil
1 cup ricotta cheese
1 (8-ounce) ball mozzarella cheese,
   thinly sliced

½ cup freshly grated Parmesan
   cheese

Heat oil in heavy skillet. Add ground round, onion, garlic, celery, and green pepper. Cook, stirring, until lightly browned; drain well. Add remaining ingredients; mix well. Bring to boil over moderate heat; reduce heat to low. Cover; simmer 1 hour.

Peel eggplant; cut into ¼- to ½-inch slices. Soak in cold salted water 30 minutes. Drain well; pat dry with paper towels.

Beat egg and water together in shallow plate. Place bread crumbs on sheet of waxed paper. Dip eggplant in egg mixture, then bread crumbs; coat well.

Heat oil in heavy skillet. Brown eggplant slices, few at a time, over moderate heat. Drain on paper towels.

In 13 × 9 × 2-inch casserole dish place layer of half of eggplant slices. Dot with half of ricotta. Top with half of mozzarella. Spoon half of sauce mixture evenly over cheese. Repeat layers, ending with tomato sauce. Sprinkle with Parmesan. Bake at 350°F 60 minutes.

braised fennel and tomatoes

Yield: 4 servings

2 small fennel bulbs
3 tablespoons butter
¼ cup water
2 tablespoons white wine

4 ripe tomatoes, peeled, quartered
Salt and pepper
Parsley, chopped

Cut off stalks of fennel; peel away stringy, pulpy outside layers of bulbs. Cut into quarters; core. Slice into thin wedges.

Heat butter in heavy saucepan until melted. Add fennel, water, and wine; cover. Simmer approximately 10 minutes, until fennel is crisp-tender. Add tomatoes. Season with salt and pepper; stir gently. Simmer 10 minutes. Place in serving dish. Garnish with chopped parsley.

stuffed zucchini

Yield: 4 servings

4 medium zucchini squash (about
   ¾ pound each)
1 pound ground beef (or ½ pound
   beef and ½ pound sausage)
¼ cup olive oil
1 clove garlic, chopped
1 medium onion, chopped
½ cup chopped green pepper

1 tablespoon chopped parsley
½ teaspoon crumbled dried oregano
Salt and pepper
1 cup fresh bread crumbs from
   French or Italian bread
1¾ cups tomato sauce (divided)
¼ cup grated Parmesan cheese

Slice the zucchini in half lengthwise. Scoop out pulp; chop.

Sauté ground beef (and sausage if used) in oil until it loses its pink color. Add garlic, onion, and green pepper; cook 5 minutes. Remove from heat. Add squash pulp, parsley, oregano, salt, pepper, bread crumbs, and ¼ cup tomato sauce; mix well. Stuff squash shells with mixture. Place in shallow baking dish. Top with remaining tomato sauce. Sprinkle with the cheese. Bake at 350°F 40 minutes.

opposite: eggplant parmigiana

breads

batter bread italian-style

This loaf is delicious served with soup and salad, or try it buttered and grilled with mozzarella cheese!!

Yield: 1 (9 × 5-inch) loaf

1 package active dry yeast	1 tablespoon sugar	½ teaspoon crumbled dried oregano
1¼ cups warm water (105 to 115°F)	1 teaspoon salt	3 cups all-purpose flour (divided)
2 tablespoons vegetable oil	¼ teaspoon garlic powder	¼ cup finely diced pepperoni

In large mixing bowl, dissolve yeast in warm water. Add oil, sugar, salt, garlic powder, oregano, and 2 cups flour. Using an electric mixer, combine ingredients on low speed. Then, increase speed to medium; beat 3 minutes. Scrape bowl occasionally. Stir in remaining flour, and pepperoni. Scrape batter down from sides of bowl; cover. Let rise in warm place (80°F) until double in bulk (45 to 60 minutes). Stir batter down. Spread evenly in greased 9 × 5 × 3-inch loaf pan; cover. Let rise until double (30 to 40 minutes).

Preheat oven to 375°F. Bake 35 to 40 minutes or until loaf sounds hollow when tapped.   Cool on rack before slicing.

bread sticks

Yield: 24

1 recipe Crisp Italian Bread (see below)	1 tablespoon cold water
1 egg white	3 tablespoons sesame seeds

Prepare Italian bread dough; let rise once as directed in recipe. Punch dough down.

Lightly flour smooth surface. Toss dough on floured surface until no longer sticky. Divide dough into 24 equal parts. Roll pieces of dough into 10-inch-long sticks. Place on baking sheets 1 inch apart. Cover with towels; let rise in warm place until double in bulk (about 45 minutes).

Preheat oven to 425°F.

Meanwhile, beat egg white and water together. Brush bread sticks well with egg-white mixture. Sprinkle with sesame seeds.

Place baking sheet or sheets (you will have to bake only 1 or 2 sheets at a time, keeping remainder covered) on middle shelf in oven. Place cake pan with 1 inch hot water in it on shelf below bread sticks. Bake 10 minutes at 425°F. Reduce heat to 350°F. Bake 15 to 20 minutes or until browned and dry throughout. Cool on rack.

Note: The process of rolling each piece of dough to form a 10-inch stick is very time-consuming, so it is wise to have help or allow a leisurely afternoon for this project. As each baking sheet is filled with bread sticks, cover it and put in a warm place to rise. In this way, all bread sticks will not be ready to bake at the same time.

crisp italian bread

Yield: 2 (12-inch) loaves

1 package active dry yeast	1¼ cups water
⅓ cup warm water	1 tablespoon coarse cornmeal
3½ to 4 cups all-purpose flour	1 egg white
2 teaspoons salt	1 tablespoon cold water

Dissolve yeast in ⅓ cup warm water (105 to 115°F); mix well. Let stand 5 minutes.

Mix the flour and salt together.

In large bowl combine dissolved yeast and 1¼ cups water. Slowly add flour mixture; stir well after each addition, to form a stiff dough. Turn out on floured board; knead 10 to 15 minutes. Add flour as necessary, until smooth and elastic. Place in greased bowl; rotate to coat surface of dough. Cover; let rise in warm place 1 to 2 hours or until double in bulk. Punch down.

Lightly flour smooth surface. Toss dough with flour until no longer sticky. Divide into two parts. Roll dough with rolling pin to 12 × 8-inch rectangle. Roll up jelly-roll fashion, beginning with a 12-inch side to form a long loaf. Pinch edges to seal. Taper the ends of loaf by rolling between palms of hands.

Sprinkle large baking sheet with cornmeal. Place loaves on baking sheet; cover with towel. Let rise in warm place until double in bulk (1 to 2 hours). With razor blade, make 3 diagonal slits in surface of loaf.

Beat egg white and water together until well-mixed. Brush loaves with mixture.

Preheat oven to 400°F. Put bread on middle shelf of oven. Place small cake pan with 1 inch hot water on shelf beneath it. Bake 15 minutes. Reduce heat to 350°F; bake 15 minutes. Loaves should sound hollow when tapped and be well-browned. Cool on rack.

opposite: crisp Italian bread

desserts

neapolitan torte

Yield: 12 servings

dough

¾ cup butter
1 cup sugar
2 eggs
½ cup ground almonds
1½ teaspoons grated lemon rind
3½ cups flour

filling

1⅓ cups raspberry jam (very thick, with lots of fruit)

glaze and garnish

2 cups sifted confectioners' sugar
2 tablespoons hot water

2 tablespoons maraschino cherry liqueur
Few drops red food coloring
½ cup whipping cream
6 candied cherries, halved

Cream butter and sugar well. Beat in eggs one at a time. Add almonds and lemon rind; mix. Slowly add flour, mixing in well by hand. Form into large ball; cover. Refrigerate 1 hour. Divide dough into 5 equal parts.

Grease bottom of 10-inch springform pan. Roll out dough 1 part at a time; cut to fit springform pan. Place 1 layer of dough on bottom section of springform pan. Spread with ⅓ cup jam. Top with another layer of dough; spread with jam. Proceed as above until all dough is used. Place ring around springform pan. Bake at 400°F on bottom oven rack 45 minutes. Cool; place on platter.

Mix confectioners' sugar, hot water, maraschino liqueur, and red food coloring to form a smooth glaze. Smooth over top of cake.

Whip cream until stiff. Place in pastry bag fitted with rose tip. Pipe 12 rosettes around edge of cake. Top each rosette with ½ of a candied cherry.

florentines

Yield: 3½ to 4 dozen cookies

½ cup butter
¾ cup sugar
3 eggs
¾ teaspoon almond extract

1 teaspoon grated orange peel
2½ cups all-purpose flour
1½ teaspoons baking powder
¼ teaspoon salt

1 cup ground almonds
1 cup semisweet chocolate chips
2 tablespoons boiling water

Cream butter and sugar. Add eggs 1 at a time; beat well after each addition. Beat in almond extract and orange peel.

Sift together flour, baking powder, and salt. Add to creamed mixture; stir well to combine. Add almonds; stir well. Refrigerate dough several hours.

Lightly grease cookie sheet.

Form dough into loaves 1½ inches wide and ½ inch thick. Make sure loaves are several inches apart, as cookies spread in baking. Make loaves as long as your cookie sheet allows, but leave at least 1 inch space between end of loaf and edge of cookie sheet to prevent burning. Bake at 375°F 12 to 15 minutes or until lightly browned and a toothpick inserted in center of loaf comes out clean. While still warm, cut loaves into ¾-inch strips and cool on cake rack.

Melt chocolate chips over hot water, stirring occasionally. When completely melted, stir in just enough boiling water to make thick mixture with consistency of layer-cake icing. Dip both ends of cookie strips in the chocolate; let dry on rack until chocolate has hardened.

italian crisp wafer cookies

Although a special iron is required to make these cookies, they are delicious and addictive! Pizzelle plates are available for many electric waffle irons.

Yield: About 3 dozen cookies

½ cup margarine, room temperature
⅔ cup sugar
4 eggs, well-beaten
1 teaspoon vanilla or anise extract

1½ cups flour
1 teaspoon baking powder
Pinch of salt
½ cup finely chopped nuts (optional)

Cream margarine well. Add sugar; beat until light and fluffy. Add eggs and flavoring; beat well.

Sift together flour, baking powder, and salt. Slowly add dry ingredients to creamed mixture; mix well after each addition. Fold in nuts. Batter should be soft and sticky.

Lightly grease pizzelle iron; follow manufacturer's directions for baking. Use approximately 1 rounded teaspoon batter for each pizzelle. Discard first 1 or 2 cookies—they absorb excess oil from iron.

These cookies keep very well in airtight container or can be frozen.

italian sesame sticks

These cookies are crispy "dunkers" and are excellent served with espresso or red wine.

Yield: 6 dozen

1 cup butter or margarine	5 cups self-rising flour
1½ cups sugar	Milk
1 teaspoon vanilla	About 2 cups white sesame seeds
3 eggs	

Cream butter with electric mixer until light. Gradually add sugar, beating well. Add vanilla and eggs, 1 at a time; beat well after each addition.

Sift flour. Add to creamed mixture; mix just until smooth. Cover dough. Refrigerate several hours or overnight.

Pour 1 inch milk into shallow pie pan. Sprinkle sesame seeds on large sheet of waxed paper. Using scant tablespoon of dough, roll on board or between palm of hands to 3½-inch long log. Dip in milk, then roll in sesame seeds; coat well. Place on greased cookie sheet 1 inch apart. Bake in preheated 375°F oven 15 minutes. Cool on rack.

Note: Any leftover seeds can be dried and toasted in the oven and sprinkled on breads or salads.

sicilian cheese-filled pastries

Yield: 30 to 35

(cannoli) pastry

cheese filling

2 cups flour	10 tablespoons white wine	⅔ cup sugar	¼ teaspoon almond extract
1 teaspoon salt	Oil for frying	½ cup flour	1 pound ricotta cheese
2 tablespoons sugar	5-inch long × 1-inch in	1/8 teaspoon salt	½ cup powdered sugar
2 tablespoons soft butter,	diameter cannoli forms	2 cups scalded milk	½ cup finely chopped candied fruit
cut into small pieces	or pieces of dowel	2 eggs, lightly beaten	1 (1-ounce) block semisweet
1 egg, beaten		½ teaspoon vanilla	chocolate, grated
		extract	

Prepare pastry. Combine flour and salt in mixing bowl. Make well in center. Add sugar, butter, and egg. Add wine; stir with fork until liquid is absorbed. Turn onto floured board; knead until smooth. Divide dough into 4 equal parts; roll on floured surface until 1/16th inch thick. Cut into 3½-inch squares. Roll squares diagonally onto forms; overlap corners. Seal with a little water.

Heat ¾ inch oil in heavy skillet to 375°F; fry cannolis, 3 at a time, in hot oil. When light golden, remove from oil; slip off of forms as soon as cool enough to handle. Let cool completely.

Make filling. Combine sugar, flour, and salt in top of double boiler. Slowly stir in scalded milk; cook over boiling water until mixture thickens. Combine 1 cup of mixture with eggs; beat well. Pour mixture back into double boiler; cook, stirring, 3 minutes. Cool; stir in flavor. (Fillng must be cold before adding ricotta.)

Beat ricotta and powdered sugar until ricotta is smooth. Fold in custard, fruit, and chocolate.

With small spatula, fill cannoli, carefully packing filling. Refrigerate until serving time.

Note: Shells can be made ahead, frozen, and filled as needed.

casrata

Yield: Serves 12 to 16

1½ quarts vanilla ice cream,	½ cup diced candied fruit	for garnish
softened	2 tablespoons rum	
1 quart raspberry sherbet, softened	3 large egg whites	1 cup whipping cream
¾ quart pistachio ice cream,	½ cup sugar	Candied fruit
softened	½ cup whipping cream	

Line 2-quart mold evenly with vanilla ice cream. Freeze until firm, preferably in 0°F freezer. Cover vanilla ice cream evenly with layer of raspberry sherbet; freeze again. Cover with layer of pistachio ice cream; freeze solid.

Cover candied fruit with rum; set aside.

Beat egg whites until foamy. Slowly beat in sugar.

Whip ½ cup whipping cream until stiff. Fold cream and rum-soaked fruit into egg-white meringue until thoroughly combined. Spoon egg-white mixture into center of molded ice cream. Spread to make a smooth bottom layer. Cover; freeze until firm (5 hours, or will keep up to two weeks).

To unmold, dip outside of mold in hot water 6 seconds; invert onto cold platter.

Whip remaining cup of whipping cream until stiff. Place in pastry bag fitted with decorative tip. Decorate with cream and candied fruit. Serve sliced.

opposite: cannoli

index

A

Anchovies and Clams with
  Spaghetti 50
Anchovy Sauce 8,70
Artichokes, Stuffed 8
Artichokes, Stuffed,
  Roman-Style 82
Asparagus Milanese-Style 82

B

Batter Bread Italian-Style 86
Batter, Fish Fry 62
Bean Soup 12
Beans and Italian Sausage 74
Beans, Romano, in Tomato
  Sauce 82
Beef
  Braised with Cloves 66
  Parma-Style 66
  Rolls with Tomato Gravy 66
  Stew 68
Boiled Mixed Meats with Green
  Sauce 80
Braised Fennel and Tomatoes 84
Bread
  Batter, Italian-Style 86
  Crisp Italian 86
  Sticks 86
Breaded Pork Chops 72
Breaded Veal Cutlets (see Breaded
  Pork Chops) 72

C

Cacciatore Chicken 36
Cacciatore Pork Chops 72
Cannelloni 20
Cannoli Pastry 90
Capellini and Chicken 36
Caper and Olive Sauce 50
Capon (Chicken), Stuffed 48
Casrata 90
Cauliflower Salad 16
Cheese
  Chicken Parmesan with
    Mushroom Marsala Sauce 40
  Filled Pastries Sicilian 90
  Filling 90
  Mozzarella Sandwiches with
    Anchovy Sauce 8
Chianti, Roast Pork in 72
Chicken
  Breast of, with Italian Ham 36
  Breast and Rigatoni 46
  Cacciatore 36
  and Capellini 36
  and Fettuccelle 44
  Florence-Style 38
  Fried, Italian 44
  with Garlic and Oil 42
  with Garlic, Rosemary, and
    White Wine 42
  Hunter's-Style 38
  Livers with Linguine 44
  Marinara 38
  Parmesan with Mushroom
    Marsala Sauce 40
  and Peas with Spaghettini 46
  and Rice Salad 18
  Roast with Rosemary 46
  with Sausage 42
  Shoemaker's-Style 40
  Stuffed 48
  Tetrazzini 40
Clam Soup 12
Clams and Anchovies with
  Spaghetti 50
Clams Casino 8
Cod with Olive and Caper
  Sauce 50
Cod, Salt, Venetian-Style 50
Cookies, Italian Crisp Wafer 88
Crab, Shrimp, and Lobster
  Diavolo 62
Cream Sauce 28
Croutons 16

D

Diavolo Shrimp, Lobster, and
  Crab 62
Dough, Pasta 28
Dough, Torte 88
Dressing 18
Dressing, Salad 16
Dumplings, Semolina,
  Roman-Style 32

E

Egg Noodles 22
Eggplant Parmigiana 84

F

Fennel, Braised, and Tomatoes 84
Fettuccelle and Chicken 44
Fettucine with Zucchini and
  Mushrooms 22
Filling 32, 34, 84
  Cannelloni 20
  Cheese 90
  Lasagna 24
  Manicotti 26
  Meat 28
  Pasta 28
  Ravioli 30
  Torte 88
Fish
  Fry, mixed 62
  Soup 64
  in Sour Sauce 58
  and Spaghetti 54
  Stew 64
Florentines 88
Fried Chicken Italian 44
Fried Squid 58

G

Garlic and Oil with Chicken 42
Garlic, Rosemary, and White
  Wine with Chicken 42
Glaze 88
Gravy, Tomato, with Beef
  Rolls 66
Green
  Noodles 22
  Salad with Croutons 16
  Sauce 80
  Soup with Meatballs 12
Gremolata 78

H

Haddock Fillets, Rolled 52
Halibut with Parsley Sauce 52
Ham, Italian, with Breast of
  Chicken 36
Hunter's-Style Chicken 38

I

Italian
  Bread, Crisp 86
  Crisp Wafer Cookies 88
  Fried Chicken 44
  Ham with Breast of Chicken 36
  Salmon Steaks 54
  Sausages and Beans 74
  Sesame Sticks 90
  Style Batter Bread 86

J

Jumbo Shells, Stuffed 34

L

Lamb
  Chops Venetian-Style 70
  Roast Leg of, with
    Rosemary 70
  Roast Roman-Style 70
Lasagna 22, 24
Leg of Lamb Roast with
  Rosemary 70
Lentils with Sausage 74
Linguine
  with Chicken Livers 44
  with Salmon Sauce 24
  Seafood 62
Lobster, Shrimp, and Crab
  Diavolo 62

M

Macaroni
  Salad with Salami 16
  with Sauce Amatrice 24
  Shrimp 56
Manicotti 22, 26
  Sauce 28
  Venetian-Style 28
Marinara
  Chicken 38
  Sauce 56
  Shrimp 56
Marinated Vegetable Salad 18
Marsala Mushroom Sauce 40
Marsala Wine with Veal 78
Meat
  Filling 28
  Pot 80
  Sauce for Spaghetti 80
Meatballs 34
Meatballs with Green Soup 12
Meats, Mixed Boiled, with Green
  Sauce 80
Melon with Prosciutto 10
Milanese-Style Asparagus 82
Milanese-Style Rice 30
Milanese Veal
  Chops 76
  Rolls 76
  Shanks 78
Minestrone, Neapolitan 14
Mozzarella Cheese Sandwiches
  with Anchovy Sauce 8
Mushroom Marsala Sauce 40
Mushroom and Zucchini Sauce 22
Mushrooms, Stuffed 10
Mushrooms and Zucchini with
  Fettucine 22

N

Neapolitan Minestrone 14
Neapolitan Torte 88
Noodles, Egg 22
Noodles, Green 22

O

Oil and Garlic with Chicken 42
Olive and Caper Sauce 50
Olives, Stuffed 10

P

Parma-Style Beef 66
Parmesan Chicken with
  Mushroom Marsala Sauce 40
Parmigiana Eggplant 84
Parsley Sauce 52
Pasta (Agnolotti) with Cream
  Sauce 28
Pastries, Sicilian Cheese-Filled 90
Pastry, Cannoli 90
Peas and Chicken with
  Spaghettini 46
Peas and Rice Venetian 32
Peppers, Stuffed 68
Pork
  Chops, Breaded 72
  Chops Cacciatore 72
  Roast in Chianti 72
Prosciutto with Melon 10

R

Ravioli 30
Rice
  and Chicken Salad 18
  Milanese-Style 30
  and Peas Venetian 32
  Risotto 30
  with Squid 60
  Tuna Risotto 60
Rigatoni and Chicken Breast 46
Rigatoni, Stuffed 32
Risotto 30, 60
Risotto Tuna 60
Roast
  Chicken with Rosemary 46
  Lamb Roman-Style 70
  Leg of Lamb with Rosemary 70
  Pork in Chianti 72
Rolled Haddock Fillets 52
Roman-Style
  Artichokes, Stuffed 82
  Lamb Roast 70
  Semolina Dumplings 32
  Vegetable Soup 14
Romano Beans in Tomato
  Sauce 82
Rosemary
  Garlic, and White Wine with
    Chicken 42
  with Roast Chicken 46
  with Roast Leg of Lamb 70

S

Salad
  Cauliflower 16
  Dressing 16
  Green, with Croutons 16
  Macaroni with Salami 16
  Marinated Vegetable 18
  Mixed Seafood 18
  Rice and Chicken 18
Salami with Macaroni Salad 16
Salmon
  Fish and Spaghetti 54
  Sauce with Linguine 24
  Steaks Italian 54
Salt Cod Venetian-Style 50
Sandwiches, Mozzarella Cheese,
  with Anchovy Sauce 8
Sardine Sauce 54
Sauce 10, 26
  Amatrice 24
  Anchovy 8, 70
  Cannelloni 20
  Cream 28

Green 80
Lasagna 24
Lemon, Veal Scallopini in 78
Lemon and Wine, with
  Turkey-Breast Cutlets 48
Manicotti 28
Marinara 56
Meat, for Spaghetti 80
Mushroom Marsala 40
Olive and Caper 50
Parsley 52
Rigatoni 32
Salmon, with Linguine 24
Sardine 54
Sour 58
Tomato 34, 68, 84
Tomato, Romano Beans in 82
Tuna 60
Tuna, for Spaghetti 60
Zucchini and Mushroom 22
Sausage
  with Chicken 42
  with Lentils 74
  Soup Sicilian 14
  and Vegetable Bake 74
Sausages, Italian, and Beans 74
Scallopini Veal in Lemon
  Sauce 78
Scampi Shrimp 56
Seafood Linguine 62
Seafood Salad, Mixed 18
Semolina Dumplings
  Roman-Style 32
Sesame Sticks Italian 90
Shells, Jumbo, Stuffed 34
Shoemaker's-Style Chicken 40
Shrimp
  Lobster, and Crab Diavolo 62
  Macaroni 56
  Marinara 56
  Scampi 56
  with Vermicelli 58
Sicilian Cheese-Filled Pastries 90
Sicilian Sausage Soup 14
Soup
  Bean 12
  Clam 12
  Fish 64
  Green, with Meatballs 12
  Neapolitan Minestrone 14
  Roman-Style Vegetable 14
  Sicilian Sausage 14
Sour Sauce 58
Spaghetti
  Chicken Tetrazzini 40
  with Clams and Anchovies 50
  and Fish 54
  Linguine with Salmon Sauce 24
  Meat Sauce for 80
  with Sauce and Meatballs 34
  Tuna Sauce for 60
  Turkey Tetrazzini 48
Spaghettini with Chicken and
  Peas 46
Squid, Fried 58
Squid with Rice 60
Steak with Tomato Sauce 68
Stew, Beef 68
Stew, Fish 64
Stuffed
  Artichokes 8
  Artichokes Roman-Style 82
  Breast of Veal 76
  Chicken 48
  Jumbo Shells 34

Mushrooms 10
Olives 10
Peppers 68
Rigatoni 32
Zucchini 84
Stuffing 76

T

Tagliatelle 22
Tetrazzini Chicken 40
Tetrazzini Turkey 48
Tomato
  Gravy with Beef Rolls 66
  Sauce 34, 68, 84
  Sauce, Romano Beans in 82
Tomatoes and Braised Fennel 84
Torte Neapolitan 88
Tuna
  Risotto 60
  Sauce 60
  Sauce for Spaghetti 60
Turkey-Breast Cutlets with
  Lemon and Wine Sauce 48
Turkey Tetrazzini 48

V

Veal
  Chops Milanese 76
  Cutlets, Breaded (see Breaded
    Pork Chops) 72
  with Marsala Wine 78
  Rolls Milanese 76
  Scallopini in Lemon Sauce 78
  Shanks Milanese 78
  Stuffed Breast of 76
Vegetable
  Salad, Marinated 18
  and Sausage Bake 74
  Soup Roman-Style 14
Venetian Rice and Peas 32
Venetian-Style
  Lamb Chops 70
  Manicotti 28
  Salt Cod 50
Vermicelli with Shrimp 58

W

Wafer Cookies, Italian Crisp 88
Wine
  and Lemon Sauce with
    Turkey-Breast Cutlets 48
  Marsala, with Veal 78
  White, Garlic, and Rosemary
    with Chicken 42

Z

Ziti with Sardine Sauce 54
Zucchini
  and Mushroom Sauce 22
  and Mushrooms with
    Fettucine 22
  Stuffed 84